Rod Gaspar: Miracle Met

All photographs are from the collection of Rod Gaspar.

Rod Gaspar: Miracle Met

by Rod Gaspar
with David Russell

BPB PUBLICATIONS
New York, New York

First Edition

Printed in the United States of America

BPB PUBLICATIONS
A Division of Bunny Prints Books
New York, New York

Dedication

I would like to thank our GOD for bringing my bride, Sheridan, into my life over 49 years ago. HE has blessed us with five great children, Heather, Cade, Corte, David and Taylor, and ten wonderful grandchildren. If it wasn't for GOD giving me the ability to play the great game of baseball, none of this would have happened. I am a very blessed guy.

I would also like to thank my parents, Betty and Lloyd Gaspar, for providing their three sons, Lloyd Jr., Jack and myself, with a loving home environment. I had a lot of support from my family. My dad was the best man I ever knew and he and Lloyd Jr. would attend my baseball games no matter where I was playing in Southern California.

— Rod Gaspar

For my parents.

"The last miracle I did was the 1969 Mets. Before that, I think you have to go back to the Red Sea."

-George Burns as God, in "Oh, God!"

— David Russell

CONTENTS

Dedication
Foreword by Art Shamsky

In Their Own Words   1
Life Before The Miracle   4
April 1969   35
Life in the City   42
May 1969   46
June 1969   57
July 1969   64
August 1969   70
September 1969   76
Winning the World Series   83
Life as a Champion   106
No Encore   110
San Diego and Hawaii   123
Life After Baseball   148
Baseball Today   193

Acknowledgments

Foreword by Art Shamsky

When I first met Rod in 1969, I remember thinking that he was this shy unassuming guy who really didn't look like a professional baseball player. That's not to mean that he couldn't play the game but more like someone who looked like he belonged in the front office as opposed to being on the field. He had that outward look of seriousness that I misread and in a very short time in 1969 I would learn that he was not shy and unassuming. Quite the opposite. And, in reality, he was a terrific baseball player. Through many times on and off the field Rod never ceased to amaze me on his knowledge of life, baseball, and things important. As a key member of the 1969 World Champion New York Mets, Rod would prove to be invaluable in the course of that year. His key hits and defensive outfield play are still remembered decades later. When people talk about the '69 Mets and that year, every player who was part of that magnificent team is mentioned. And Rod Gaspar is right there with everyone else. I chuckle to myself when I think about Rod's bold prediction that he shouted out to everyone who would listen right before the World Series in 1969 that the New York Mets were going to win four games in a row against a terrific Baltimore Orioles team. And, even though we lost the first game of that series in 1969, we did go on to win the next four in a row. Incredibly, he was right! We did win four in a row. Just one example of his brashness and confidence. To this day I still tease about his appearance on the television show "The Dating Game" along with teammates Ken Boswell and Wayne Garrett. I always tell him, 'Not one of you three had any personality to speak of,' and yet when it was time to pick her date the girl picked Rod. We never stop laughing about that show.

But Rod Gaspar is more than just a former Major League baseball player who once made a bold prediction. He is a devoted husband, father, and grandfather, and a terrific person. Through his faith Rod has dealt graciously with the highs and lows of life, with personal tragedy and continues to be a person of the highest qualities.

I make it a point to speak with Rod as often as I can. The time we spent together as teammates on a very special memorable team will always bind us together. And, decades later I'm happy to say I still cherish his friendship.

This book will give you some terrific insight to the man, Rod Gaspar. While I know him on a different level and am honored to call him my friend, I am sure you, the reader, will find out so many more interesting things about him.

Enjoy!

Art Shamsky

Rod Gaspar: Miracle Met

In Their Own Words

Keith Olbermann: It is amazing that 19 of the "Amazin' Mets" of 1969 got on base, or were involved in plating a run, or pitched an inning, in the five-game World Series upset of the impossibly-favored Orioles. The run that broke the Birds' back in Game 4 came home on one of only 23 sacrifice bunts ever executed by J.C. Martin. Light-hitting Al Weis was their second leading RBI man in the Series. Ron Taylor, who never had more than 14 saves in a season, salted away Game 2. Nolan Ryan, who had four saves in his life, got one of them in Game 3, while relief ace Tug McGraw never got out of the bullpen. Ryan could never have guessed that though he'd pitch until 1993 his World Series career was over, while Tom Seaver couldn't have conceived that the victory Martin's bunt would bring him would be the only one he'd ever get.

Just as remarkably Rod Gaspar scored exactly 36 runs in his entire major league career, but the one in the '69 Series is among the most famous of all time. That's the kind of team the '69 Mets were. And the play in which Gaspar scrambled home from second through the shadows on that Martin bunt had one other touch of trivia to it: I was there, up in the left field mezzanine with gigantic binoculars straining to figure out what chaos was unfolding before my eyes when Baltimore's Pete Richert picked up that bunt and plunked Martin square in the back with it. It was my first World Series game and those names Martin and Gaspar left my 10-year old fan's soul buzzing for months. I wouldn't meet Rod Gaspar until 40 years later, but he was a delight, and just as happy to hear my memory of that game as I was to tell it. It cheered me further when he handed me his business card, which turned out to consist almost entirely of a reproduction of his 1970 baseball card, something I remembered as vividly as I did that game.

I would wind up seeing twelve World Series games from inside the dugouts as a TV reporter, another 20 or so from the press box, and 25 more from some very nice box seats and not one of them has stayed with me the way Rod Gaspar's big game did.

Jerry Koosman: Rod, though not a regular in the lineup every day, was indeed a very valuable player on our ballclub. He was there to not only root on the team when he wasn't playing but had the ability to fill in in many different positions. He played when someone else needed a rest or got hurt, pinch-hit whenever Gil needed him. He pinch-ran for some players so we would have more speed on the base paths. His versatility gave us depth and more strength. Gil had a third sense in being able to keep every player on the team ready for any situation. Rod was always ready and always in great shape. He was a pleasure to have as a teammate.

As a utility player, you don't always get the accolades you deserve from the press, but the team knew how valuable he was to help make us winners. But above all of this, he was also a Christian on God's team!

Someday, I hope I can get his autograph!!!!!

Kooz.

Bobby Pfeil: I first met Rod when I joined the Mets in June of 1969. He was kind of a perfect fit for the 1969 Mets: Young, enthusiastic, could play all three outfield positions, switch-hit,

2

and ran well. Rod was one of us younger players with Wayne Garrett, Duffy Dyer and myself. It was a unique team in the sense that we all played. Rod was enthusiastic. They all filled a role. The veterans accepted that and the young guys knew their spot. We share something pretty special.

Ron Swoboda: In 1969 most of us learned that the only time everything that everyone does matters is when you win it all. Rod Gaspar will always be one of us. The World Champion 1969 New York Mets.

Life Before The Miracle

If it wasn't for baseball I wouldn't have anything. Really. I don't know what kind of life I would've had. Who knows if I'd still be around? Growing up, all I wanted to do was play baseball.

I was born at St. Mary's Hospital in Long Beach, California on April 3, 1946. We moved to Compton. Duke Snider was from Compton. And Don Rowe, who later pitched for the Mets, was from there.

A few years later my family moved to Lakewood. The address was 4523 Albury Avenue. I'll never forget that address. This was just after the war and there was a brand new city being built, so we moved there in '51. The two-bedroom house cost $8,000 to buy. Can you imagine that? It was a nice area, a middle-class neighborhood. Lakewood was one of the first planned communities.

I had the best parents you could have. Lloyd and Betty Gaspar were down-to-earth, humble people. To me, my dad was the best man and most respected man I ever knew. He was a hard-working iron worker which is probably the hardest labor work there is. And he did that for over 40 years.

I realized how hard it was when I worked with him a few years in the offseason during my pro career and he put me out there with the laborers. It was hard work but I enjoyed it. He was amazed how I could work all day and not get tired. I was starting to like that iron work but then I'm looking at all these

35, 40-year-old guys who are bent over and I'm thinking, 'No, I don't think so.'

There were a lot of neighborhood kids. Two neighbors were Skippy and Skipper. They were both a year older than I was and we would play all the time. I always used to beat up Skippy and Skipper. I'd get in fights with them. One time I beat up Skippy and he went home crying. His dad told him, "Go back there and beat up Rodney." So he came back to our house and I beat him up again.

Being in Southern California, my dad and I would listen to Dodgers games on the radio. My dad liked listening to them because of Vin Scully calling the games. So my dad would come home from working, go in the backyard, turn on the radio, and have a glass of Jim Beam while relaxing and listening to the game.

At an early age I had an interest in sports, like most kids. I was the middle boy of three, and we all liked sports, preferably baseball. My parents were very supportive of that, with my dad coaching us. I admired my dad more than any man I ever met. He wasn't real tall, about 5' 9", 140 pounds but he was very strong and very athletic. He had that fire in his belly. He was so supportive over my lifetime of my interest in sports. He attended every game he could, even if it was two hours away. And when I was younger my dad would help out coaching whatever team I was on, even though he never played baseball. He always provided well for us. We had the best of the best sports equipment. Everybody loved Lloyd.

Lloyd Jr. helped me and was a good high school outfielder and first baseman. Lloyd Jr. was the same as my dad. He would go with me to whatever games he could. There were times he would drive two and a half hours by himself to watch me play baseball. I don't think many brothers would do that. You don't think about it at the time but he would be out there really watching me. There was one time that I was laughing at something that happened during a game and he made a comment to me about laughing on the field. It ticked me off and I was ready to go fight him but he was right. Lloyd Jr. was a good baseball guy and knew his stuff. My mom attended my games as well as my brothers' games. She was athletic as well, and fortunately I inherited some of that. She was a good golfer and bowler. Both of my parents were well coordinated. We couldn't have had better parents. We had a good life and were spoiled like a lot of kids are, but we never messed with the old man. He was a tough little guy. There was one Christmas when I was a kid, and we had our mother's relatives over. My dad didn't really care for some of these people, and he got in a hassle with this one guy. My dad knocked this guy through the screen door. And this is Christmas. It's supposed to be a joyful, nice happy time. And he knocked this guy through a door. That's just how he was.

My dad and his brother, Red, had always gotten into fights while growing up during the Great Depression. Uncle Red had actually been an amateur fighter and could hit really hard. My dad would tell stories about the two of them being at Jordan High School in Long Beach and getting in fights. There was one guy who was a tough guy and a dirty fighter, and he fought Red. And this guy was holding his own and then he kicked Uncle Red in the groin. Red goes down and he tells my dad not to let that SOB get away, to hold him until he got back up. So I guess they waited and my uncle gets up and beats the crap out of this guy. They said if Red hadn't been stopped, he would've killed the guy.

We didn't particularly like our next-door neighbors in Lakewood. My mom didn't really talk to them. One day, something happened while my dad was working under his truck. And the neighbor comes over and made some comments about me and my brothers. Again, that's the wrong guy to mess with. My dad came from out under the car to confront the guy, and by the time he came out, the neighbor ran home. Another time, the neighbor sent over his son, Walter, to fight Lloyd Jr. And my brother kicked his butt. That's the kind of environment I grew up in. Scrapping and fighting. And I was the scrappiest of the three boys. As I get older, I try to avoid that stuff. It's not worth it. But when you're younger, you react to situations stupidly. It doesn't solve anything, but it happens.

I wasn't very big but GOD blessed me with athletic ability. So growing up I was always competing with the bigger kids in Little League and the pony league. I was a left-handed third baseman in a midget league because I was the only one who could throw the ball from third to first. This means I had to field the ball, pivot and fire it. As a 12-year-old, I was an All-Star in my Little League and we won our local championship but we didn't get invited to nationals. I never did understand that. We had three guys who signed professional contracts. Three out of 12 isn't bad. Jim Strickland, someone I grew up with and still say in touch with, was a pitcher with the Twins and Indians in the '70s. Bob Schellenberg played a couple of years in the Phillies system and then got smart and went to school.

Growing up, I was a Yankees fan and of course Mickey Mantle was my favorite. I met him when I was selling insurance and had a picture taken with him. I always thought Mantle was a really big guy. He wasn't tall but he was thick. I was taller than him and I'm six feet tall. But he was thicker. Mickey was such a strong guy.

I made All-Star teams, but as I grew older I was still small. My buddies were six, seven, eight inches taller than me and I'm competing against these guys. And to make it worse, I developed an ulcer when I was 13. I used to worry a lot about dying. This one guy who was a couple of years older than I was, Art Tweedy, ended up getting leukemia and dying. That always bothered me.

Before my parents knew it was an ulcer, I thought I had leukemia. I heard my parents talking one time and I heard something about "two weeks." When you're a whacko at that age, all kinds of things go on in your brain. I heard them say "two weeks" and I thought I had two weeks to live. That's how messed up I was at age 13.

Finally, I found out I had an ulcer. Up to that point in my life, before I got sick, I was always cocky, real confident. I was very aggressive playing sports. I'd fight kids all the time. That was the combative nature I had. I maintained that until I got my ulcer. After that ulcer I lost all confidence in myself and in my abilities.

By the time I was in high school, I was 5'2" and weighed 105 pounds, fighting the "little man's complex." At 15, I flunked my learner's permit twice. I finally got that, and when I went to get my driver's license, I also flunked that twice. You think I had a bad attitude? I was a ticked-off little guy.

This is how I messed up I was. I would walk past people, and if they didn't notice me, I'd be all worried that people didn't like me. You go through that as a teenager. Those are tough years for kids. I used to struggle going to sleep at night because my mind would be racing, worrying about things. It doesn't do any good to worry. Somebody said 99 percent of the bad things you worry about never happen anyway, so why worry about it? But for a few years it was a struggle for me.

There was one time in junior high school when I was sitting and a ball hit me in the face. I turned around and while still holding the ball, I was having words with this guy. And this guy punched me right in the nose. My dad always told me the cardinal rule in a hassle was to get the first punch in. Don't let the other guy hit first. This guy nailed me right in the nose.

One night when I was a teenager, I came home late and tried to sneak in the back door. My mother is there waiting for me with a clothes hanger. She tried to hit me with it and she ended up hurting herself trying to swing the thing at me. She was fiery. She would come after people. My dad would say that she couldn't break an egg but she wasn't afraid of anybody. She would mouth off to anybody, which got her in a lot trouble.

The next few years, I still played sports although I still didn't have a good attitude. My sophomore year, I was playing "c" basketball, which was the lowest division they had. Finally, between my junior and senior year of high school, I grew seven inches and made the varsity basketball team. I also played varsity baseball, but I wasn't anything special. I was 5'9", 135 pounds, just starting to come into my own. I was still competing with the bigger guy. I wasn't better. It's not like I was all-league, but I was OK. I had this drive, a killer instinct. I may have it more now because I understand it better than I did then. You have somebody down and you want to beat on them. I was so aggressive playing basketball. I used to foul out of games all the time. I averaged four fouls per game.

I was the same way in baseball. I was always looking to take the extra base, thinking about scoring from second on a fly ball to the outfield. When I would slide into a base, I would try to knock the ball out of the fielder's glove. I would try to break up double plays. If I was in a rundown, I would definitely try to knock the ball out of somebody's glove. I would throw a forearm at them to try and knock the ball out. You could do that then. I don't know if you could get away with that in today's game. Running down the first-base line, if a guy got in my way, I would throw that forearm to knock the ball out because I wasn't big enough to knock him over. I watch these guys now who hit a ball down the first-base line and the pitcher comes over and the guy just stops and lets the pitcher tag him. And I say, "What a pussy." I didn't play the game that way. That's the way ballplayers were then. At least I was. I wasn't going to let anyone tag me out. Like when Albert Belle ran over Fernando Vina. OK, that one was over the top. Looking back, I'm surprised no one kicked my butt for trying to knock the ball out of their glove, but thankfully that never happened.

I was a right-handed hitter but when I was 13, I started experimenting with hitting left-handed, which was an advantage because I had the breaking ball coming into me instead of going away from me. It took me five years until I was a solid left-handed hitter.

I was humbled by that ulcer and 'the little man complex.' I think it's good that we are humbled, that way we can learn from it and keep going without quitting. Quitting is easy. Anybody can quit. Even now, in my 70s, I'm still as competitive as I was when I played ball. It's just crazy. That little man complex still sticks with me. It fuels my anger and makes me focus more on winning.

While playing junior varsity baseball, I learned a lesson about quitting in my sophomore year of high school. I was playing left field and I went to field a ball which I misjudged and it got through me, and I just dropped my head and stopped. There was a runner on base and I kind of dogged it as I went to retrieve the ball. I went after it nonchalantly. In other words, I quit.

The ball rolled to the fence and the coach, Chuck Schildmeyer, took me out of the game which taught me a big-time lesson: You never give up on anything in sports, which I didn't after that. Never give up, never give in.

It's good he took me out. One, that's bad baseball on my part and two, it's a bad example, because you don't know who's watching in the stands. What if there was a scout watching and thinking, "That Gaspar's a dog. He doesn't hustle at all."

Coach Schildmeyer took me out and he did the right thing. I respected him for it. If I can remember it over 55 years later, you know it stuck in my brain. Chuck was a good guy. Coaches of young players have to instill that mindset. Now you watch major league games and guys run half-heartedly to first, or a hit falls in and they get a single instead of a double and the manager doesn't do anything about it. Unfortunately, if a manager did do something about it, the agent of that player would be on his case. It's very frustrating to watch that. I think it's a privilege to play sports. Some people wish that they signed even if it was just to play in the minor leagues but I think it's good to just move on with your life.

Very, very, very few guys sign and even fewer get to make it to even Double-A. If you can get to Triple-A, that's really good. And if you get to the majors, that's excellent. It's funny how someone can be a stud in the amateurs only to never be heard from again. How about the kids who dominate in Little League and never play after high school because they are the same at 17 as they were when they were 12? When I played Little League, I was 4'10" and I would bat against this 5'10" pitcher named Johnny Martinez. He could throw hard but I battled him. But he never really grew after Little League. He was so much bigger but then he just remained at 5'10". You always wonder what happens to these guys.

Remember that some guy who plays a few games in the majors and bats under .100 is still one of the best in the world. Isn't that something?

I played at Lakewood High School. Dave Marshall had gone to Lakewood. He would become a Mets reserve outfielder after yours truly was sent down to the minors in 1970. Tony Muser was the first baseman on my high school team. He was a very good defensive first baseman. Tony played for a while in the majors and eventually managed the Kansas City Royals.

The baseball team had a bunch of guys that made it to the pros. Muser was signed as an amateur free agent by the Red Sox. Catcher Bob Schellenberg played in the Phillies organization. Jim Strickland was our star pitcher, and he signed with the Dodgers right out of high school in 1964. He was probably the best pitcher in the California Interscholastic Federation that year. Jim played for 11 seasons in the pros, including a few years with the Twins and Indians. We had Tim Lane, a shortstop who could really hit. Lane was taken by the Angels and played in the minors although he didn't make it above Single-A. He had all kinds of injuries. Les Mundel was a big pitcher who threw hard. Les played four seasons in the Angels organization, and was the winning pitcher in the Midwest League All-Star Game one year. Jim Parks was a pitcher who was named the 1962 CIF Player of the Year, the season Lakewood High School won its first title. He didn't make it far in the pros because he didn't throw hard, but he was a control pitcher who knew how to pitch.

Five of the nine guys in the starting lineup made the pros. That's pretty good. It's funny that I'm one of those five, and that the other four guys were probably better than me at the time.

Our teams didn't have all the good players. We faced some talented opponents as well. Mike Montgomery went to Millikan High School. He coached college basketball for over 30 years, and led Stanford to the Final Four in 1998. Long Beach Poly was one of the best athletic schools in California, really one of the best in the country. Not just in baseball but basketball, football and track. They had Ollie Brown who was the first pick in Padres history, and played for six teams in the majors over a 13-year career. Ollie also played basketball in high school. He was in an athletic family. His brother, Oscar, played with the Atlanta Braves for a few seasons. In the same family was Willie Brown, who played a couple of seasons with the Rams. Bob Wiswell, a left-handed pitcher who played at Poly, eventually signed with the Braves and made it to Double-A ball. Bob Bailey was a guy who was a few years older than me so I never related to him, but he was 1961 CIF Player of the Year at Wilson High School. Bailey was a bonus baby with the Pirates and played 17 seasons in the majors.

During my sophomore year, Lakewood won the title but I was still on the junior varsity team. My older brother had played varsity baseball, so the coach knew me. So there was some name recognition which helped me. Artie Boyd was the nicest guy in the world and a good baseball man. He was admired by the guys on his team. He coached at Lakewood from when it opened in 1958 to the 1970s.

We had good teams my junior and senior years but we didn't win anything. Not a league title, not CIF playoff games, not anything.

There was great competition which helped me. It's better than just being far and away better than everybody and going to the next level and falling behind. Plus, I had some ability. If you don't have ability, it doesn't mean anything anyway. Then when I got bigger, I could play with these guys and became a better ballplayer than any of them.

I enjoyed my high school days. There were times I preferred basketball over baseball. My high school basketball coach was Jerry Mitchell. He's still active and teaches people to swim in Florida despite being in his mid-80s. He was a heck of a baseball and basketball player in his day. My last year playing for him was the last season he coached.

People knew me in school but I wasn't really popular. But they knew me as the little guy. I didn't really date in high school. The only so-called girlfriend I had watched me play basketball in the CIF playoffs and she wanted to meet me afterwards. That game was against Pius X, the top seed in the playoffs. They had some really good players, including Rick Adelman, who played and coached in the NBA. We lost to them.

Those CIF playoffs ended with Pious X facing Long Beach Poly in the finals. Long Beach Poly had Gene Washington as a forward, before he was a four-time Pro Bowl receiver on the 49ers. He used to jump center. He was shorter than the center, Mel Reed, but he was an athlete. Mack Calvin was the sixth man on that team and went on to play in the pros. Mack was a five-time All-Star in the ABA. Like I said, there was a lot of talent in the area in all sports. Poly beat Pious X with a late comeback. I loved when we played Poly even though those guys were so much better than us.

Anyway, I ended up with this girl after our playoff game, which was the same night Cassius Clay upset Sonny Liston to win the heavyweight title. I hooked up with this gal for five weeks and then she dumped me. I didn't know she had a boyfriend and he came back from wherever he had been, and she broke up with me. That was my only experience with dating or being a social person. I didn't join any clubs; I didn't like to dance. My high school days weren't the most exciting. The most famous event that happened was that Clay-Liston fight, which was going on at the same time as the playoff game. So the biggest event was a boxing match that I didn't even see.

My focus was sports, just baseball and basketball, but mainly baseball. That was my whole thing. I had no other plans in life. I wanted to be a baseball player and thankfully I was. Sports can come naturally to some people, and others can still learn. A tennis instructor said that his philosophy was if you buy an ice cream cone and put it in your mouth, you can learn to play, but if you stick it on your forehead, your chances aren't as good.

In the classroom, I was a fine student with a B average. I don't remember any of my teachers, other than the coaches. Math was my favorite subject until I went to college and took calculus. That was a whole new ballgame. It wasn't trigonometry or geometry or algebra. It's a whole different animal. Whoa. What am I doing here?

I didn't have any colleges recruiting me when I was in high school so I went out for the baseball team at Long Beach City College. I started developing and getting stronger. I wasn't playing much at the time, but finally the coach got smart and started using me. It was one of those things where things just started clicking. As my dad would say, "Katy, bar the door," nothing was going to stop me. I was 18 or 19 and that's when I took off. Then I started advancing past my teammates. I was a little bigger, a little stronger and my natural abilities took over. I started hitting well from both sides of the plate. Switch-hitting was such an advantage for me. My confidence increased dramatically. Baseball really helped me get out of that depressed, no-confidence attitude I had had since age 13. It took me that long to really get my confidence back. If you really want to accomplish something and you have the ability and the confidence to do it, you can get it done. As the centerfielder at Long Beach City, I led the team in hitting was named MVP.

Joe Hicks was my coach at Long Beach City College. He was a wonderful man and I learned more baseball from Joe Hicks than from anybody. He studied the game, he was smart, and he would see the fine details of the game. He taught me about the mental part of the game, the relaxed concentration. Joe was very creative, always thinking and he had a great personality. He was also an actor, who appeared in a number of shows, including an appearance on the "Andy Griffith Show" as a baseball coach. Joe was a good looking guy, about 6'2". He was even the Marlboro Man at one point. Joe took a leave of absence from the school, and then returned to win a few more titles. He passed away from cancer in 1991.

I was also in the California Collegiate League in 1965 and 1966, on a team sponsored by Mike Salta Pontiac. Joe Hicks was the manager of the team. We had Andy Messersmith, who was a four-time All-Star and led the National League in wins one year. He started his career with the Angels. It seemed like so many of those California guys ended up signing with the Angels or Dodgers.

On that collegiate league team, I was in the outfield with Mike Floyd and Barney Scholl. Floyd played in the Angels system, and Scholl was in the Yankees organization for one season. I was in right, while Mike was in center. I thought I should be playing in center. I got to go to Dodger Stadium as part of the summer collegiate league all-star team. John Lowenstein, who played 16 years in the majors and won a World Series with the Orioles, was an all-star. So was Brent Strom, who was the pitching coach for the Astros when they won the World Series.

Also on the all-star team was Bill Seinsoth, a player most people have never heard of. He went to USC and was the Most Outstanding Player of the College World Series in 1968. Bill was a first baseman who eventually signed with the Dodgers organization. Bill died in a car crash in 1969. His college coach said that had it not been for that tragedy, he would have been the first baseman of the future and people would not have known Steve Garvey as the first baseman of the Dodgers.

In the offseason, I would play for a local team at Blair Field, where Long Beach State plays games now. I played with a team called the Long Beach Rockets. A former ballplayer named Jack Graham ran the team. He led the Pacific Coast League in homers one year in the 40s but he was beaned, and after that he was afraid of being at the plate. I was a young guy on that semipro team. We had Buddy Pritchard, who had played second base for the Pirates. Buddy had been a star at USC and signed with Pittsburgh as a "Bonus Baby". He would go into second base and would try to tear the shortstop's head off when trying to break up a double play. These guys played hard-nosed baseball and I learned from that. I learned how to play the game from watching these older guys. They had tobacco all over their face and their uniforms. You have guys

17

trying to take out infielders in semipro games in the winter, and that stuck with me. It was a good learning experience for me. I really took off as a player in 1965 and 1966.

From Long Beach City College I went to Long Beach State College on a scholarship. They were the first four-year school to show interest in me although I later learned that some other schools, including USC, were interested. I played there in 1966 and 1967. By then, I was one of the best college baseball players in the country. I did well at Long Beach State College. Playing college ball helped me develop as a ballplayer. I knew I was going to play professionally. Now when people ask me, I recommend that they go to school, especially if they can get a scholarship to a four-year school. If they have the talent to sign professionally that will happen eventually. Go to school first. Long Beach State had produced one major league player before me. Dick Nen was a first baseman with a few teams in the 60s and his son, Robb, later became a pitcher for the Marlins and Giants.

Whitey Herzog watched me in college when he was working for the Mets. We had a game against USC and the opposing pitchers were Bill "Spaceman" Lee, the future Red Sox starter, and Tom House, the future pitching guru. They combined to shut us out on three hits, and I had two of them, one off each guy. I was on first, and I wanted to run. Both pitchers were lefties. I'd tick coaches off sometimes because I'd run on my own. Well, they both picked me off first base that day. I wasn't even caught stealing. They picked me off. But Whitey liked that because he knew I was aggressive and that I wanted to steal.

My last game at Long Beach State College, we had a doubleheader scheduled. Mr. Wuesthoff (who I still call Mr. Wuesthoff for some reason) wanted me to sacrifice bunt in the first game. I'm thinking, Man, I want to get a base hit. I tried to drag bunt for a hit and made an out instead. And he took me out of the game. Nowadays, they don't take the kid out of the game or anything. Not that they know how to bunt either. But that showed you the kind of guy he was. I was the best player on the team but he didn't care. I respected him but I thought forget him and I started chewing tobacco. And I got sick. He didn't plan on playing me in the second game anyway, so that's how my college career ended, getting sick on tobacco.

I had been drafted by the Mets in 1966. I had decided to return to school, and then they drafted me again in 1967. By then I was very confident, very self-assured, and very cocky. I knew I was good.

I had some outstanding amateur coaches. Funny thing is, when you go pro you think you're going to get all this great coaching and learn so much but in California we had great school coaches. I played for Artie Boyd at Lakewood High School, Joe Hicks when I was at City College, and Bob Weusthoff at Long Beach State College. Mr. Weusthoff was a good man, very personable. He knew his baseball and was a nice man who was also very competitive. I never heard him (or Artie Boyd or Joe Hicks) say one cuss word in all the years I was around him. And there was also John Herbold at Long Beach Poly High School who was the smartest baseball guy I ever met in my life. John was a Stanford grad. He wasn't very tall, only about 5' 9", but he was loud. I think he knew more baseball than anybody I had ever been around, even though I knew him as an opponent as he was coaching at Poly high school. He loved the game and studied the game and he would do things that other coaches wouldn't do. It's like anything else in life. If you enjoy it, you'll probably be pretty good at it. He was a winner. He won a Southern Sectional title at Poly in 1963, and then came to Lakewood and won titles in 1970 and 1976. Herbold won over 450 games as a coach at Cal State Los Angeles. You've got to have talent to win but coaches can make a difference. He knew how to communicate with his players. We would play his teams, so we never liked him because they always beat us. And Herbold was out there and always loud. But I got to know him later on and he was just the nicest guy. He once gave me an official National League baseball. Sadly, John passed away in the summer of 2017.

Back then, before I signed, I am glad I had coaches who helped me to understand the game because I didn't get the coaching I thought I would get in the minor leagues other than Whitey Herzog, the Mets director of player development. Once I got to the majors, the Mets had a great staff which included Gil Hodges and Yogi Berra, but in the minors you better learn the game or you're going to be in trouble because the competition for your job is incredible.

You don't realize how good you have it until later in life when you look back and realize we had some really good amateur coaches who knew baseball.

I knew I was ready to go pro, so I turned down some more amateur opportunities. I could have played for the Alaska Goldpanners, a collegiate summer baseball team. Tom Seaver played for them at one point. One of the things they're known for is a Midnight Sun Game. The sun is out for almost 24 hours, so they traditionally play one game that starts at 10:30 at night. And I was also asked about the Pan-American Games, which would have featured the best college players in the country. But I turned down those choices.

What's funny about the Mets drafting me is that they never spoke to me when I was in college. Other teams, including the Braves, talked to me, but I didn't think about the Mets. They drafted me in 1966 and wanted to give me $10,000. I didn't sign because I wanted more money plus I wanted to go back to school anyway. My parents hadn't seen $10,000 in their lives. They were upset that I didn't sign. "How could you turn that money down?"

Then they drafted me again in 1967. Gary Gentry and I signed that year. I was the number two pick of the Mets and Gary was number three. Rich Folkers was number one. I wanted $20,000 to sign. As a 15th-round pick the previous year, the Mets offered me $10,000, so I went back to school. Then they drafted me again the next year as the second pick and I figured, Heck, I'll get my $20,000 now. I was ready to go out and play and they knew it.

You know what they offered me? The same $10,000. That really irritated me. Gary was picked behind me and he got $20,000. I guess he was a better negotiator than I was. They knew I was ready to play and they had me. Obviously, Gary deserved his money. I ended up signing for a $12,000 bonus. The scouts that signed me were Nelson Burbrink, who later served as the Mets scouting director and director of player development, and Dee Fondy, who was a first baseman for years with the Cubs and the last batter in the history of Ebbets Field.

Gentry wound up as my roommate on the road. When we were roommates, he was already married and had a baby. In college, he was at Arizona State and I was at Long Beach State and we went to Arizona to play them in Tempe. Gentry pitched against us and we beat him. I had a couple of hits off him. That was Gentry's only loss of the year and Arizona

State ended up winning the College World Series, and Gary was player of the year.

I got along great with him. He had a lot of self-confidence in his ability. He could throw the heck out of the ball. All you have to do is ask Brooks Robinson, who was surprised in the World Series by how well Gentry threw. He was very confident and I think he wanted to be the next Tom Seaver. Who wouldn't want to be? Gary hurt his arm a few years later and that was that.

I'm so happy that I played sports. If I didn't play baseball I don't know what I would have done. I have no clue. I had always wanted to be a baseball player. Some guys top out at age 12. The big kid in Little League that's hitting home runs at age 12 and all of a sudden at 15 he's not playing baseball anymore. Some will top out at 15, others at 18. I was one of those guys who got better as I got older. Even after I signed, I was getting better and better.

A good example is Daniel Nava, who I watched play in the outfield with the Angels and won a World Series with the Red Sox. I recently read a story about him. He was a team manager of the baseball team at Santa Clara after he failed to make the team as a player. He loved the game, he hung in there, and finally he got a chance to play a little bit and the guy took off. This guy never quit, never gave in, never gave up and that's the way I was.

Signing with a team that was in last place every season helped my chances of making the major leagues faster than it would have if I signed with a pennant winner with a loaded outfield. The 1967 Mets actually used 54 players during the season, which is such a high number. They were looking for viable players. I think they were getting tired of bringing in former stars that were past their prime. And it worked. They went from using over 50 players and losing over 100 games in 1967 to winning the World Series by the end of the decade.

I signed on June 8, 1967, and went to Williamsport, Pennsylvania to play at the Double-A level in the Eastern League. That Williamsport team had three 1969 Mets: Me, Gary, and Jim McAndrew.

The manager in Williamsport was Roy Sievers, who had been a five-time All-Star. He let you play ball and didn't say too much. He was a better hitter than anybody on the team. He was in his early 40s but he could still hit. He would take batting practice and hit rockets. I knew about his accomplishments, that he led the American League in homers and RBI one year. I'm a history guy anyway. I like biographies, not just sports biographies, and I looked into him. I didn't talk to him about it. There was no doubt Roy was underrated because he spent his best seasons on the losing Washington Senators. And he won American League Rookie of the Year when he was with the Browns.

There was one game where he chewed me out in the clubhouse after I made an error which scored the winning run for the other team. He just hammered me in front of everybody, just embarrassed me. I didn't say a word but I told myself nobody would ever do that to me again.

The ballpark in Williamsport was terrible. In fact, all the parks in the Eastern League were bad. You couldn't see at night. The Pirates and Cardinals actually played a game in Williamsport in 2017, and the Mets and Phillies did it in 2018. They did it as a tie-in with the Little League World Series. I had attended the 1967 Little League World Series because they wanted to have a couple of guys from the Williamsport Mets. Ted

Williams was there although I didn't get to meet him. It was a much smaller event than it is today.

The lights were just bad when I played there. I hit .260 and was in the top 10 in the league. There was one .300 hitter in the league, Bernie Smith, our third baseman. It was a real pitchers' league. There was one time in Pittsfield, where I was leading off the top of the first and the sun was coming down directly in centerfield. You couldn't see. We had to delay the game until the sun went down. Those were the kinds of parks we had.

When I got to the team, they told me I would play right away. That was the first lie I heard in baseball. I didn't play for a week and I was going crazy sitting on the bench. The centerfielder was Jon O'Dell. You talk about cautious. My goodness, he wouldn't go for anything. They said he was a really good defensive outfielder as he never made any errors. I could see why. He didn't go for anything. Finally Sievers got smart and put me in the lineup.

After my first week in Williamsport, I got a check for something like $87. I thought, 'Gee, I got paid for nothing.' I was just sitting on a bench.

I had my first-at bat in Reading, Pennsylvania against the Phillies club. It was late in the game and I was going to pinch-hit for the pitcher. I was going to pinch-hit against Robin Roberts. The guy in front of me made the last out of the inning and that was the last hitter Roberts ever faced. He retired after that. I would've gotten my first at-bat against a future Hall of Famer, but it didn't happen.

About two months into that season, something just clicked in my brain. It was the weirdest thing. It was like a light went

24

on. At that point I started understanding the professional game of baseball. It's so much different than amateur ball because you're playing every day and the players are better. I was starting to figure out things and how to adjust to the professional game. You have to adjust or you're not going to make it. If you're a psycho and you're worried about every little thing and get ticked off and can't focus, then you'll have a problem. An example is Billy Beane, the Oakland GM. He was a top prospect but he admitted he didn't have it mentally. But he became an excellent general manager.

We had a good group in Williamsport. Curtis Brown was an outfielder who was in the minor leagues for a long time and played one game with the Expos. Duffy Dyer was the catcher. Edward Gagle was the bespectacled third baseman. You think the guys strike out a lot now? Edward struck out all the time. If he didn't strike out, he'd hit a home run. He hit .188 with 13 homers and struck out 158 times that season. He'd get so mad. Gagle also made 16 errors at third.

Denny Lundgren was similar at first. He hit 18 homers and struck out 109 times while making 15 errors at first base. He was a little less than six feet, but he was built like Mickey Mantle. Eighteen home runs in the Eastern League are pretty good.

Sherman Minster was the second baseman and later became a blackjack dealer in Las Vegas. He would always have poker games with the guys. John Gonsalves was the shortstop. He went to Long Beach State College before I did. He didn't hit much. They called him "clang" because when the ball was hit to him it would clang off his glove for an error. It was funny because when he played amateur ball in California he was always considered to be a good fielder. He went on to coach Long Beach State College for nearly two decades.

Wilbur Huckle was an infielder on the Williamsport team. What a classic. I'm telling you the truth here. The ballgame would be over and he'd be in the clubhouse, showered, dressed and out of there in five minutes. Nobody knew where he went. "Who knows where old Wilbur went?" He was a scrappy player. If he was in a rundown, he would purposely get in the path of a throw so he could get to the next base. He was fearless. I tried to track him down recently in Texas but I had no success. He's just as elusive as he was when he played baseball.

The pitching staff included Ed Bauta, a Cuban who had pitched for the Cardinals and Mets, and was towards the end of his career. Jay Carden won 13 games and had an ERA of 1.69. He would be traded to Montreal in 1969 in the Donn Clendenon deal. Carden never made the big leagues. The Mets had some top prospects in minor league baseball like Carden, Jerry Johnson and Al Schmelz. And there were Gentry, McAndrew, Koosman and Jon Matlack all on the way up.

Bill Hepler was a left-handed pitcher who threw straight overhand. He had the most immaculate uniform I've ever seen on a guy. He made sure the shirt had no wrinkles as it was tucked into the pants. There were no wrinkles anywhere. He was a perfectionist when it came to putting on his uniform. Jerry Hinsley was a right-hander from Texas who also threw overhand. Al Schmelz was another hard thrower. Hinsley and Schmelz both got called up to the majors for a bit at the end of the season. Schmelz is now building homes in Scottsdale, Arizona. We had Bob Johnson who was a good pitcher who was with the Pirates in the early 70s. Darrell Sutherland was a tall, lanky reliever with a three-quarters delivery who had pitched for the Mets in the mid-60s.

We went 73-66. Then I went to the Florida Instructional League, where all the top prospects were sent. I had started school again but had really wanted to go to Florida and dropped out after a few weeks. I had left college because I was in class thinking about how I wanted to get on the field.

I met some of the other top players. One of the young prospects working his way up the system was Ken Singleton. He was a New Yorker, a little different than the other guys. I thought he had an air about him, but he was a player. We were both cocky guys. We got into a discussion and he said he was going to outhit me, and I said, "You're not going to outhit me, big boy; I'm going to outhit you. I'll hit for a higher average than you." And I outhit him. I batted .306 and he finished with a .245 batting average.

So I outhit him although he accomplished a lot more in the game than I did. Kenny was a good ballplayer. He was big, a strong switch-hitter with a strong arm in the outfield. He was on those excellent teams in Baltimore with Eddie Murray. He's been announcing Yankees games for about 20 years.

Ken Boswell, Duffy Dyer and Danny Frisella were on the team. Greg Goosen was the catcher. The Goose and I roomed together for a little while. I never saw him. Casey Stengel once said that 'Goosen was 19 and that in 10 years he had a chance to be 29.' Greg became good friends with Gene Hackman, and even became his stand-in for movies. His brothers are involved in boxing in California. His older brother, Dan, is the main. Greg was very personable and funny. People liked him wherever he went. Greg was a real pull hitter. I saw him once pull a ball over the third base dugout. Greg could pull anybody. He died too young, from a heart attack a few years ago.

Teddy Martinez, who would play on the 1973 Mets team that won the pennant, was with us in Florida. Bobby Heise was a Mets prospect who went on to play in the infield with seven teams in the major leagues. Joe Moock was a third baseman who played for the Mets for a few weeks at the end of 1967. He never really made it because he fought himself too much. His temper would take control of him. Heise and Moock were two of the many players that the Mets tried at third base in the early years of the franchise.

After the season, the Mets had arranged for me to get into the service, but I flunked the physical. If you were in the Reserves, you were less likely to be sent to fight in Vietnam, and some Mets, like Bud Harrelson, would be in the Reserves each summer. There was that ulcer I had at age 13 plus I had a history of sinus problems. So they classified me 1-Y. I guess they didn't like to imagine me sneezing everywhere while I'm in a swamp in Vietnam. I don't think that would go over very well.

Then in 1968, the Mets moved their Double-A team to Memphis, so I went there. That upset me because I thought I should be in Triple-A Jacksonville. Gentry was promoted but I wasn't. I was hot about that.

I thought moving to Memphis was no big deal because baseball is baseball but I'm glad they made the move. I had a good year, led the league in hits and made the All-Star team. I hit .310, which was 50 points higher than I had hit in Williamsport, although I thought I had been better the year before. The air was thinner in Texas. I also liked the Texas League more because we got to fly. In the Eastern League we had to sleep on buses, which is never fun.

I was in good shape. I took this drink, called Nutriment, so that I could add weight because I was so skinny at 22 years old. Playing in a game every single day, I weighed around 155 pounds. So Nutriment would help me keep weight on. I was doing well, so some guy gave me a motorbike. When you do well, people are nice like that. I almost got killed on that thing. There was one night I was leaving someone's house, and this dog started chasing me. I made it to my motorbike but then I had trouble getting it started. Fortunately, I eventually got it going and rode away from there.

Roy Sievers was the Double-A manager again. We had a game in Arlington, Texas which I was late to, so he didn't have me in the starting lineup for the first time all year. I was ticked. I was hot. He used me as a pinch-hitter late in the game and I got a base hit. I'm on first and we're down by one. The other team brings in a lefty pitcher, Paul Doyle. In the dugout, our catcher Lloyd Flodin yells out at me, "Rodney, this guy has a great move to first. Don't get picked off." Yeah, yeah. Right.

I'm off the bag by about three feet and all of a sudden the ball is in the first baseman's glove. It was the best move I've ever seen. So I ended that rally. We ended up losing the game and in the clubhouse Sievers just lit into me.

He and I went at it, firing f-bombs at each other. He said, "I'm going to call Whitey and send you out of here. You're gone." I was fine with that. We were going back and forth. The guys in the clubhouse knew my temperament and thought, Oh geez, here we go. I was playing well and leading the league in hits. "Go ahead and call Whitey and say whatever you want."

The next day I go to the park and I'm in the starting lineup. I guess you can get away with that when you're a prospect. I never had another problem with Roy. He was a good guy.

Sometimes you get caught up in things. I wasn't in a good mood because I had been benched. But it blew over and that was it. He never said anything about it again, and I didn't bring it up either.

The team did get in a fight with Arkansas, the Cardinals affiliate. Something happened and we all came on the field. And there were punches being thrown. It wasn't a typical baseball fight where some guys just come out and hold each other back. Most of the so-called baseball fights are just players cussing at each other. Arkansas had a pitcher, Santiago Guzman, who nearly got me. I turned around and all of a sudden I see this big fist coming at me. Thankfully I ducked. If he blindsided me, he would've knocked my head off. I don't know if there's a safe spot on the field during those fights.

Tim Foli, who had been the overall number one pick that year, played a few games in Memphis. Rich Folkers, who had been the number one pick of the team in 1967, pitched in Memphis. Roy Foster was an outfielder with a good bat. Mike Jorgensen was there in Memphis and made his major league debut that year. David Schneck, a young left-handed hitting outfielder, was on the team.

Barry Raziano was a pitcher from Baton Rouge. Barry was kind of an ornery guy. I heard he was at a party and Miss Memphis or some pageant winner was there and started razzing him. Raziano ticked her off and she had a frying pan and threatened to hit him with it. So he did something and she smacked him with it, and he cold-cocked her. He knocked her out right there.

After that season the Mets wanted me to play winter ball in Culiacan, Mexico, which I did. OK, no problem. I didn't know what it was like. I almost didn't get out of the place.

LIFE BEFORE THE MIRACLE

This was just two or three weeks after the season ended in Memphis. They told me I'd have a week to get in shape before I started playing. I get down there and the general manager picks me up at the airport, and drives me to where we're playing Hermosillo in a doubleheader. I'm there fresh off the airplane and they've got me in the starting lineup. And I'm not in shape. I'm an American guy. I guess they wanted their money's worth. Of course I wasn't hitting for the longest time. But I got in shape and started hitting well and finished over .300, like I normally did back then. Being there was a whole new lifestyle for this kid from America and I did not like it. It was a tough area and there were very poor people. The owner of the team was a rich Chinese-Mexican man. He didn't like me and I didn't like him. I remember going into his office and asking for a raise. I think he ended up giving me a small one. I didn't know any of the players and I didn't care to get to know any of them. Playing in Puerto Rico might have been different because I heard that was a great league. The team knew I didn't like it there but I still played well for them and was the best player on the club.

In fact, the manager of the team told me, "I don't like you, but I like you as a ballplayer." He was direct and honest, which I appreciated. I didn't always care for him, but the manager was a good guy. He played me in every game. Of course they had to play the Americans to get their money's worth. And I was glad that I went because I hit well and it kept me in shape for the spring training in 1969.

After the season was over, I'm getting ready to leave and they held me up. They wouldn't let me go. I asked what was going on and was told that the other American on the team (they were allowed two) apparently had some drug issue but had already left the country and they wouldn't let me go until I paid for his bad behavior, whatever that meant. I think he was a pillhead. So I had to pay somebody in the organization to get out of Mexico. I thought, This is the last time I'm ever coming to this country.

Nothing against the Mexican government or the people, because the people were real nice, but if you have a bad experience it sticks with you. And it was the last time I went there until our daughter was married in Cancun, and I didn't really want to go to that. But that was a whole new environment and was one of the nicest places I ever stayed in my life. It was great. You were in your own little world there.

During the 1968 offseason the Mets put me on their 40-man roster. I was considered a prospect and was invited to spring training. I had worked out year-round, and was in good shape, so I was ready to play ball. I went in with the idea that I was going to make the ballclub. That was always my mentality.

Unfortunately, the Mets didn't know that much about me outside of that I had a good year in 1968 and that they had to protect me on their 40-man roster or risk losing me to another club. So I go to spring training and they give me a high number, 57, which basically meant they didn't expect me to make the ballclub.

I went to spring training just with the idea of making the ballclub. I wasn't even thinking about how the club might do that year. I wasn't concerned about that. First of all, you have to make the club. I knew I could make the club if I was just given the opportunity.

I was impressed with the coaches. There was Gil Hodges, our manager, from the old Brooklyn Dodgers. I think a lot of us were in awe of him. We didn't want to upset him or have him mad at us. We kind of had a fear of him, but it was a fear of letting him down that comes from respect, as opposed to fearing that he would scream at us or attack us if we messed up. I think we all had that. And as the season would go along, he kept making great decisions. He was in charge and we were going to do what he wanted us to do. And we knew what we had to do. He didn't have to say too much to us.

And of course Yogi Berra, an all-time favorite who was such a nice man, was our first-base coach. All the other coaches were super. Eddie Yost, our third-base coach, was a wonderful guy. Joe Pignatano, our bullpen coach who grew tomatoes in the bullpen at Shea Stadium. Rube Walker, our pitching coach, was a former Brooklyn Dodger catcher. We had a great coaching staff and they all got along well, just like the players. I was happy to be associated with nice people. The New York Mets were a class organization in 1969.

One day, I was sitting in the stands in St. Petersburg with Wes Stock, the Mets minor-league pitching coordinator who had pitched in the '60s with the Orioles and Athletics. He went on to become a big league pitching coach with Oakland and some other teams. We were watching the Mets play at Al Lang Field and I was irritated because they hadn't given me any chance at all to play. Cleon Jones was in left, Tommie Agee was in center and Ron Swoboda was in right. And they had Art Shamsky. They were all veterans of the game. Tommie was AL Rookie of the Year with the White Sox in 1966. The Red Sox actually thought about trading Carl Yastrzemski for Agee straight up. Cleon had been in the big leagues as far back as 1963 and hit well. He almost hit .300 in 1968. Swoboda had hit 19 home runs as a rookie in 1965. Shamsky had been in the big leagues for a few seasons and came over from Cincinnati.

And here I am with Wes Stock, saying, "I should be out there. I'm as good as Jones. I'm as good as Agee. I'm as good as

Swoboda. I'm better." That was my attitude. The way I look at it, that's the attitude you have to have if you're going to be a professional baseball player or a professional anything in life. You've got to know you're good and I knew I was good. Unfortunately, they didn't know I was that good because they really hadn't seen me play. I wasn't real happy.

They were planning on sending me down to Triple-A Jacksonville because not many guys make the big leagues after less than a year and a half in the minor leagues, especially back then. A few days later the Mets were getting ready to go on a road trip and Art Shamsky was taking ground balls at first base when he hurt his back. Art had had a history of back trouble anyway. It took its toll on him and hurt his numbers with the Reds before he was sent to the Mets.

Art couldn't make the trip, so Gil took me, started me, and I went on a 14-game hitting streak. I did everything. I hit a home run, I drove in runs, I scored runs, and I stole bases. They were, in a sense, forced to keep me. I was having a great spring and the sportswriters were writing it up in the newspapers back in New York. I found out I made the team on my birthday, April 3. They gave me number 17, which is now the number our grandchildren wear when they play ball.

April 1969

I started the season with the Mets batting second and playing right field. I had played quite a bit toward the end of spring training, so I figured I'd be in the Opening Day lineup. It was Tommie Agee, Rod Gaspar, Ken Boswell, Cleon Jones, Ed Charles, Ed Kranepool, Jerry Grote, Bud Harrelson, and Tom Seaver.

Before the game, Howard Cosell called me over for an interview. I forget exactly what the question was but he asked me a dumb question and I gave him a dumb answer. Then he asked me something to the effect of "how do you think you're going to do this year?" And I go, "I'll try to do the best I can." That was it. He shut it off and walked away. He didn't say anything else. So that was my big interview. Is that like Cosell or what? Maybe he was still ticked off because the Mets hadn't hired him as an announcer when they first started off in 1962. The Mets sure did the right thing when they hired Hall of Famers Lindsey Nelson, Bob Murphy, and Ralph Kiner, all great guys and wonderful gentleman...probably the best decision they made, next to hiring Casey Stengel as manager, in the early years of the Mets.

It was the first time I had ever been to Shea Stadium. It was so big, and could hold over 55,000 fans. It was very exciting and I was fired up.

We were playing the Montreal Expos in their first-ever game. In my first at-bat against Mudcat Grant, I hit into a double play. Tommie Agee had singled, but then Grant jammed me and I hit it in the air to short where Maury Wills made the catch and doubled Agee off first. The next inning, with Grant already out, I singled off Dan McGinn. I don't have the ball. I wish I had more things from those days, like a lot of players do. Later in the game I had an RBI single off McGinn. In the sixth, I drew a walk against Don Shaw, and then stole second although I was stranded. I lined out against Shaw to end the eighth, which looked like it would be my last at-bat of the day.

Instead, I went 2-5, scored a run, knocked in a run, stole a base and ended up striking out to end the game. And I very, very seldom struck out. We had scored four times in the ninth to cut the lead to 11-10. Duffy Dyer hit a three-run home run. Amos Otis and Agee singled to bring me up. Carroll Sember came into the game to pitch to me. If I had never faced a guy before, I wasn't going to swing at the first pitch. We had the tying run on second, the winning run on first. I worked the count to 2-2. He threw me a sinker (maybe a spit ball?) down and away to strikeout me out. I usually fouled it off or put it in play. That continued the Mets streak of not winning an Opening Day game in their young history. We would win the World Series before we won an Opening Day game.

The next day, we got our first win. I drew a walk against Bill Stoneman and singled off Mike Wegener in the 9-5 win. The final game of the series was the game where Tommie Agee hit the only upper deck home run in the history of Shea Stadium. I was in the on-deck circle watching it. It was a low fastball. He got that big head of the Adirondack bat on it. Tommie used a big bat, about 36 or 38 ounces. A lot of guys now use 30, 31, maybe 32 ounce bats. I believe he was the strongest guy on our team. That homer was hit a mile high and just kept going. They later marked the spot where it landed. The game wasn't televised, so the highlight hasn't turned up on YouTube or anywhere.

Lefty pitcher Larry Jaster was the one who gave up the homer. Agee hit another homer off Jaster later in the game. Agee was five for eight with four home runs off Jaster in his career. I don't know if Jaster ever hit him. Maybe he should have. In those days they would. Nowadays they don't. I went hitless in four at-bats that day, but we won the game.

Then St. Louis came in for a three-game series. I had three hits against Steve Carlton in the opening game. Years later, a book came out with all these hitter pitcher matchups, and it turned out I was four-for-seven against Carlton with a walk. That's a .571 average. I had two singles and a double in the first meeting. It's one of those things where Carlton probably doesn't even remember me hitting him like that. And I didn't remember it until I read it in that book.

I always played hard. But that early in the year, I was excited to be on the ballclub and try to contribute to winning. I was trying to stay on the ballclub because we had some great talent in the minor leagues. I was concerned about playing well so I could stick with the Mets.

I was hitting well in the first week but then I had an 0-4 game against Dave Giusti and was 0-3 with a walk against Bob Gibson. Gibson had won the Cy Young Award the year before with an ERA of 1.12. We lost both games to complete a sweep. They should've kicked Gibson off the mound after he walked me.

Gibson was an intimidating guy. Can you imagine some of these hot dogs now who watch where they hit the ball and flip their bat? As a pitcher, I would drill them the next time up, there's no doubt. Gibson would watch guys after they hit a home run to see if they showed him up. If they did or didn't, he would go after them the next time up. When Mickey Mantle hit a home run, he would drop his head and run around the bases. He didn't want to show the pitcher up plus he didn't want the guy getting mad at him and hitting him the next time up. That's a sign of respect. The Mick did it right. These kids celebrating now, if they did that against Drysdale, or Gibson, or Seaver, or Ryan, they'd get drilled. It was a different mindset then, and I liked it. I think if a guy tries to show you up, it's OK to bust him in. But it doesn't happen very often in today's game.

After the Cardinals series, we went to Philly for our first road games. I singled off Woodie Fryman but we lost the first game. Then I had another hitless game, with a walk, against Chris Short and Gary Wagner, although we got back in the win column. We went to Pittsburgh for a two-game series after that. Bob Moose held me hitless in four at-bats and the Pirates won 11-3 over Koosman. The next day, I had a bunt single against Jim Bunning in the sixth but was caught stealing in a 1-0 game. I also made a throwing error a few innings later.

I didn't think anything of my struggles at the plate. I had gone 0-4 in the minor leagues before but I was in the big leagues now. I was a rookie, and Gil sat me after that. After starting the first 10 games, I sat out for the next four. Although I would play in 118 games, I wasn't an everyday player anymore, which was tough for me at the time because I was hyper. It was tough to sit in the dugout and watch a game. As a rookie, if I wasn't hitting consistently like I had been in the minors and spring training, it was just a matter of time before I would be benched. If I was a veteran it might have been different, but I was on and off the bench for the rest of the year. I never was a regular starter after that. I always felt that if I had been in the big leagues for a few years, I would've stayed in the lineup. Because I was a rookie, Gil sat me down. You don't take chances with first-year guys when they get in a slump. I didn't feel like I was in a slump but I was hitting .231 after 10 games, which explains it. It kind of surprised me, but I didn't know any better because of my inexperience. But I played well enough that I stayed with the Mets all year and wasn't sent to the minors. Future All-Star Amos Otis was sent down, but I wasn't.

Gil was a great leader. He wouldn't scream but he was tough one-on-one. He called me in his office one time after I had a confrontation with our clubhouse guy Nick Torman. I was just a rookie and mouthing off to Nick about something. So Gil called me in his office and tore into me. He let it out. He didn't hold back. The whole time he was talking (or yelling), I looked him right in the eye. I got the message.

We had Cleon, who hit .340 that year, Tommie hit .271, plus there was Ron in right. Art Shamsky hit .300 and his Spring Training injury was the only reason I made the club (GOD bless Art). We hit .242 as a team the entire year. I wasn't happy with sitting because we all want to play. Nobody wants to sit. But Gil knew what he was doing. He was a lot smarter than I was. I am not complaining. After all, we won the World Series

I started smoking cigarettes during the season, at least once I wasn't in the starting lineup. I began smoking because I was hyper and didn't like sitting on the bench. Some guys would go to the clubhouse or the runway to have one. I'd grab a Marlboro and go down to the runway leading to the clubhouse to smoke during the game. I smoked throughout most of my professional career, even though I would only have one here and there. But I would smoke a few during the game and nobody thought anything of it. Not many guys smoked.

I sat for four games, and then pinch-hit for Tom Seaver and flew out against Ferguson Jenkins in a loss to the Cubs. I faced a few future Hall of Famers in my first three weeks. They were tough. But they're all tough. I don't care who it is. You have to have talent to pitch in the big leagues.

I remember Juan Marichal getting me out and he was throwing pitches right down the middle. It was as if he was saying, 'Here rookie, hit this.' He was throwing me nothing special, but he got me out. And why not? First time facing me, seeing if I could hit his stuff, and I didn't.

We lost again to the Cubs and Bill Hands, while I grounded out as a pinch-hitter. He would knock guys down and he seemed to go after Agee for some reason. But he was a good pitcher.

We split a doubleheader with the Cubs on the 27th. The Cubs took the first game with a four-run ninth and a Randy Hundley home run. Phil Regan, The Vulture, pitched the bottom of the ninth. Sandy Koufax called him "The Vulture", when Phil was with the Dodgers, because he would come in late in games and try to clean up the mess. Phil was the unsung hero of the 1966 Dodger team that won the pennant. He was 14-1 with 21 saves and a 1.62 ERA. Phil became a coach and later managed the Orioles for a season.

In the second game of the doubleheader, I led off in the bottom of the ninth in a scoreless game. I reached on an error by the left fielder and made it to second. Nowadays, if there's a pop-up to the left fielder, the guys don't run it out and if it's dropped they end up at first base. You better run balls out hard under Hodges or he'd sit you down real quick. Now the players don't run as hard and the manager does nothing. A few batters later, Cleon Jones hit a three-run homer off Rich Nye to win the game.

Then we went to Montreal for the first time. It was real cold. They had gas heaters in the dugout at Jarry Park. The cold is what I remember most about Montreal. You can imagine swinging the bat in that cold weather. If you don't hit it right, your hands are going to hurt like heck. As a 23-year-old new to the major leagues, you try not to think about the weather. I tried not to pay much attention to it when I played. But if you're sitting in the dugout, that's a different story. You're not moving around. But we learned to adapt. The first game there we beat Mudcat Grant, who had started against us on Opening Day. Grant was a former two-time All-Star who had helped the Twins win the American League pennant in 1965. He was towards the end of his career and only played 11 games with the Expos. I was hitless in three at-bats and was hit by a pitch.

On the last day of April, we entered the ninth inning tied 1-1. I led off with a single off Mike Wegener, which brought up Ken Boswell. Donn Clendenon was the Montreal first baseman, and he was edging in, expecting a bunt. I noticed he was leaving the bag early and I stole second. I basically stole it on my own. Then Boswell failed to bunt me to third but drove me in with a hit to right and we won 2-1. That was a heads-up play on my part. Gil noticed it ahead of time and so did I. Anytime you get an edge like that, you go. I always was a good base runner. Before he was a Hall of Fame manager, Whitey Herzog was the director of player development for the Mets. He helped build the farm system that we had. He mentioned one time that I was the best base runner in the organization. You take advantage when you can, and that one paid off because we won the ballgame.

Mets record at end of April:
9-11, 5.5 games out of first

Life in the City

One day, I went to Jack Dempsey's Restaurant. Dempsey had been the heavyweight boxing champion from 1919 to 1926. He was my favorite fighter of all-time. I was a huge boxing fan. Maybe it was because I was always in scraps growing up. I would always buy Ring Magazine to keep up with the boxing news. So one day I walk in, and the first thing you see is this big mural of Dempsey's fight against Jess Willard in which Dempsey won the title. I asked somebody where Mr. Dempsey was. And they said, "Well, you just walked past him." When I opened the door and walked in, he was sitting right behind the door. I went over and introduced myself, although I didn't tell him that I played for the New York Mets. I just said, "Hi, Mr. Dempsey. I'm Rod Gaspar."

He was born in 1895, so he was 74 at the time, and he was still an imposing man. He was a mean-looking man. Dempsey was a well-dressed man with a nice suit and tie and all that, but he was still imposing. I wouldn't have wanted to mess with him even at 74 years old. I had always wanted to meet Jack Dempsey. He was very cordial. That was one of my biggest thrills. I should've told him I play for the Mets, but I think I was awestruck just meeting him.

I play some of his fights on my VCR. I'd tape fights when they came on TV, even the replays of old fights with Joe Louis, Rocky Marciano, Ezzard Charles and Jersey Joe Walcott. I even go back to James J. Corbett and Robert Fitzsimmons, which was one of the earliest fights ever filmed. I've got

42

footage of Jack Johnson fighting Jim Jeffries. I like those old fights even though I don't like seeing a guy get hurt. I don't like when a referee doesn't stop a fight as soon as he should. This UFC stuff is crazy to me, getting a guy down and elbowing him. You know these guys are going to have their brains scrambled.

But I know all about those old boxing matches, including the one where Dempsey beat Willard. Willard was the champion and was so much bigger than Dempsey, just towering over him. And just before the bell rang for the first round, Dempsey's manager, Jack "Doc" Kearns, told him he beat the whole purse that Dempsey would win in the first round. Dempsey knocked Willard down seven times in the first round, but the bell rang before Willard could be counted out. Dempsey won the title when Willard couldn't come out for the fourth round, but didn't get any money for the fight. There are stories about Dempsey's gloves being loaded, or having brass knuckles or a metal bar in his right hand. Or did Kearns put plaster of paris in the tape as he wrapped Dempsey's gloves up? Willard had teeth knocked out, his jaw was broken, and he was so beat up. To this day, nobody knows for sure if anything was done illegally in the fight, and I certainly didn't ask Mr. Dempsey.

There was one night in May when we had an off day, and I went to Madison Square Garden to watch a welterweight fight between Emile Griffith and Stanley "Kitten" Hayward. That was the modern MSG, which had moved to its current location the year before.

Most night games were at 8:00. There wasn't much exciting stuff going on in the mornings. I'd go to a diner for breakfast. I would get to Shea Stadium between four and five unless I wanted to take some extra batting practice. It seemed like the coaches were always there ahead of everybody. Once we're there, I'd sign baseballs for fans, get ready, go out, run, throw, take batting practice, take infield and outfield, then go back to the clubhouse for another half hour and wait for the starting pitcher to get warmed up. The games would be over by 10:30, so I'd leave and try to get into bed between one and two in the morning, and then do the same routine the next day. I was living in Manhattan with Kenny Boswell. It was a little, dinky place where we were paying $400 a month, which was a lot of money for me at the time. I didn't last too long in Manhattan.

There was just too much activity in Manhattan, although it was funny to people watch in the city with all the oddballs and characters in the area. It wasn't my kind of place, although whenever I go back for reunions I really like it. It wasn't like I couldn't go down the street without fans stopping me, because nobody really recognized me. But I didn't sleep much because I was out and about so much. I had to get out of there so that I could play some decent baseball the next day. I was a single guy, so I didn't stay in one place for too long.

I had to get out of there, so I went to live in Queens. I moved to Forest Hills after I met a guy named Miles Asness who owned a nightclub-type place. He was a real nice guy who let Wayne Garrett and I stay in a place he owned. And we'd go to Miles's nightclub after games before going home. Free rent, free car, and free gasoline. When you win, everybody loves you and wants you and things are taken care of. When you do well, people want to do things for you. (And that doesn't just go for New York. It's true anywhere.) People want to be around you.

I didn't ride the buses, although I would take the trains. Of course there was the 7 train that people took to Shea Stadium. I remember getting off that thing and people were just roaring off the subway. Everybody is always in a hurry. There was some poor older lady I saw, and this guy just rushed into her and knocked her down. There was just no regard for anybody. It's terrible how everybody is always in a rush in New York City. You'd get in a cab and the drivers would constantly be honking the horns. It's crazy to be in that environment. New York City is just a different place. Period. It didn't really shock me, but it was different than anything I had ever seen. I remember being at an airport for some event, and this guy is there with his family, and the dad is just yelling and screaming at his kid in the middle of the airport. He was just going nuts. I thought, Give me a break. How can people be this way? There were plenty of obnoxious people there, but there are obnoxious people everywhere.

Meal money was good. I believe we got $25 per day. You could eat real well on that kind of money 50 years ago. Today, they probably get more money for one road trip than I made in a whole year. We had chartered flights, which were real nice, not like the long bus rides you would need to take in the minor leagues.

May 1969

We lost to Montreal to begin the month. I was 1-5 with two strikeouts but I did throw Coco Laboy out at third on an 8-5 double play. A few innings later, Laboy hit the game-ending sacrifice fly to me.

Then we went to Wrigley Field for the first time that season. I liked those old parks like Connie Mack Stadium and Forbes Field. Forbes Field was actually the last stadium Babe Ruth played in when he was with the Boston Braves, and he hit three home runs in one game with one going over the roof. Crosley Field in Cincinnati was old. Heck, they were all old. The only ones still around in the National League are Wrigley Field and Dodger Stadium. Dodger Stadium was one of the newer ones, opening in 1962. The clubhouses were a lot better than they were in the minor leagues. It's hard to compare them to anything because at the time they were the best ones available. But it doesn't compare to what these guys have now. I was reading that the one in the new Yankee Stadium has a swimming pool and a weight room. I thought our clubhouse was nice at Shea Stadium. It was one of the newer ones back then.

At Wrigley Field we had to go up stairs to get to the small clubhouse. It was terrible. And as you'd go up the stairs, people would be yelling at you, cussing at you. In the pre-game warm-ups they'd be throwing stuff at you, just hammering you. The fans in San Francisco were the same way. The fans out there may have been a little worse, yelling and screaming. These people, man. Get a life.

I don't get these people. I guess they think if they buy a ticket they can say whatever they want to professional athletes. Well, I disagree. They're so wrapped up in sports. They're crazy. Some of them should be locked up in a mental institution. Some guys relish playing on the road. Al Hrabosky, the reliever known as The Mad Hungarian, said that his goal in life was to get a standing boo.

We lost the first game at Wrigley even though I had an RBI single off Ken Holtzman. Gil had me hitting third. Can you imagine that? I had never hit third in the minor leagues that I remember. I had a sac fly off Ted Abernathy and a bunt single in the ninth off Phil Regan to bring the tying run to the plate but we lost 6-4. The next day I went hitless against Fergie Jenkins and the Cubs won a duel between Jenkins and Nolan Ryan, although Regan got the win and Cal Koonce got the loss. There was Regan again, picking up the garbage.

We took a doubleheader from them, with Seaver and Tug McGraw winning both ends 3-2. I scored a run in both games. Tom Seaver always treated me well even though I didn't really hang around him. He had a vibrant personality. He was obviously the leader, even at age 24. Playing behind Seaver was great. And Nolan Ryan was another good guy, low-key. I didn't know how good Nolan would become although I knew he threw the ball harder than anybody but he was a little wild, which was an advantage for him because opposing players were afraid to hit off him. He was a stud and proved it in the World Series. I loved playing behind those guys.

Tug was a nice guy, always smiling. He was a very funny guy. Tug once said he would spend 90 percent of his money on good times, women and Irish whiskey, and that he would probably waste the rest. He was a bit off-kilter like a lot of us are. He had actually started pitching for the Mets in 1965, and was the first Met to beat Koufax. But 1969 was his first real steady year he did consistently well. A number of years later, we were at a card show and after the show was over, Tug wanted to see a friend, Bernie McGrenahan, who was an entertainer in Manhattan. He asked if I wanted to go and I said sure, so we saw his friend perform and we got to spend some one on one time together, which was nice. We didn't hang out that much during the 1969 season.

Tug could've been an entertainer. There was some event a few of us were at, and he was kind of like the emcee and just had everybody cracking up. He was a smart guy too. He sure knew how to pitch and had a great screwball. There was a function in the '90s, where he brought his son, Tim McGraw, to the hotel. Tim had the song "Indian Outlaw," which was one of his first hit songs, and we got to meet him. Tim was actually born during the 1967 season and didn't know Tug was his real dad until he was a teenager. Of course, Tim McGraw turned out great and has done very well for himself. I believe when Tug had his health problems with his brain tumor, he lived on Tim's property in Tennessee.

I loved the way our pitchers worked. Get the ball, throw the ball. We didn't have these four-hour games like they have now. Two and a half hours was a long game for us. Our pitching staff didn't mess around. Now because of computers and analytics, guys have too much information in their heads. I don't watch it much because it's so boring. Now they have the intentional walk where you don't have to throw four balls. That's to speed up the game? Give me a break.

Part of the reason our pitchers didn't mess around is because Jerry Grote wouldn't let them. Jerry was a tremendous defensive catcher. Seaver pitched to Johnny Bench when he was with Cincinnati and Carlton Fisk when he was with the

White Sox. Those are two Hall of Fame catchers. And Tom said Jerry Grote was the best defensive catcher he ever pitched to. Grote was very competitive and was continually fired up. The guy would get so irritated. I remember him coming in the dugout after a base hit and he was ticked off. I have no clue why. Obviously, it didn't affect his playing. He was an excellent catcher.

Sometimes during a game, the pitcher wouldn't throw the ball where Grote wanted them to and he'd take the ball and rifle it back to his pitcher harder than they threw it to him. One time he was doing it to Koosman, and that's not the guy to mess with. He threw a rocket back to Jerry, and Koosman called him out and said, "Hey, if you do that again I'm going to kick your butt." Grote got the message and didn't do it again because Kooz could take care of himself. Grote always had that fire in his belly, which was good. To me, you can't teach 'fire in the belly'. It's just that sometimes Jerry got a little too fired up. But that's OK. You'd rather have a guy like that than the opposite.

We had good pitchers not named Seaver, Koosman, Gentry and Ryan. Jim McAndrew was a very talented starting pitcher. He pretty much stayed to himself. Years later, when I would go down to the Mets Fantasy Camp in Port St. Lucie, Florida, Jim was there and could still throw the ball well at age 60. Ron Taylor was very reliable out of the bullpen. He was a quiet guy, Doctor Taylor. He later became the team physician for the Toronto Blue Jays. He was a great relief pitcher who knew how to pitch. He relieved Jerry Koosman with two outs in the ninth inning of Game Two of the 1969 Series to get the save. He was also a member of the 1964 World Series champion St. Louis Cardinals. Don Cardwell was a wonderful man from North Carolina. He threw a no-hitter with the Cubs in 1960. Don was a big, strong, tough guy. I really liked his family. I met them at the wedding of his granddaughter a number of years ago in Monterey, California.

There was Cal Koonce, another quiet pitcher. He was a tremendous Christian man who pitched a lot of years in the big leagues. He only played two more years after '69. He became the head baseball coach at his old school, Campbell University. It was tragic that he died in the early '90s of leukemia. He was the first '69 Met player to die. He was 52.

The pitching was also helped by good defense when they weren't striking guys out. The team put together a good infield. We had Ed Charles at third base. Ed is great. He signed in the '50s and went through a lot of racial strife and prejudice. He was a big, big Jackie Robinson fan. When the movie "42" came out a few years ago, they had a kid playing Ed that looked up to Jackie. There was also a recent TV special about Jackie which Ed was in. Ed Charles is a sweetheart of a guy. They called him "The Glider" because he was smooth as silk, relaxed playing his position, a real good third baseman, and had some power. He is a very, very nice man and is a poetry buff. He's written a lot of poetry. He wrote one book, which I still have a copy of. He was one of the older guys on a team with young guys. We could've fielded a team of guys under 25 if we had to. Ed was 36 and 1969 was his last year in the big leagues. What a way to end a career, a World Series champion.

There was also Wayne Garrett, the left-handed hitting third baseman and youngest guy on the team. He was 21, and, like me, had never played in the majors before 1969. We were both single and occasionally hung out together in the city. Wayne was a good ballplayer and a good guy.

Bobby Pfeil, another rookie, also saw a good amount of time at the hot corner. Bobby had the game-winning bunt single in Montreal on the day that that Neil Armstrong and Buzz Aldrin walked on the moon. Bob lives in Northern California and he and his company have done very well in the real estate business. We talk to each other often.

Ken Boswell was the left-handed hitting second baseman. Ken and Art Shamsky would hang around Mr. Laffs. It was a sports bar and restaurant owned by Phil Linz, the former Yankee and Met. That was their place. Over the years I've stayed in touch with Boswell. He's in the Austin, Texas area. I have invited Boswell to visit my wife and I in California. He won't leave Texas. Those Texas boys like their Texas.

Al Weis had been acquired in the trade with the White Sox that brought Tommie Agee to the Mets. Al was a solid, solid ballplayer. He didn't say much but he sure knew how to play the game. He proved that against the Cubs with a pair of home runs at Wrigley Field. And he also proved it in the World Series. Donn Clendenon was the MVP but Al won something called the "Little MVP" and was awarded a Volkswagen.

Bud Harrelson was at short. Bud, who was actually born on D-Day, missed some time during the 1969 season because of military service and Al Weis did a great job of filling in at shortstop. Bud was an excellent defensive shortstop and the best shortstop I ever played with. He could make contact and put the ball in play. He started the season at 155 pounds and ended the season at 135 pounds. He couldn't keep any weight on because he played all the time. He was a very smart, heads-up player. And Bud went on to spend many years in the organization as a player, coach and manager.

We had Ed Kranepool at first base. The Krane. He was the Mets' original bonus baby. He played every year for the Mets, even at age 17 in 1962. He is another nice guy. They all treated me well. I was a rookie but they didn't do much of that hazing stuff. Krane looked so much older than me. He looked older than any of us but he was only 24 at the time. Maybe that was from playing in New York. I don't know. But he could hit and field. He was good friends with Swoboda, and with McGraw, whom he roomed with on the road.

Ron Swoboda was a very competitive ballplayer, who made himself into a very good outfielder in 1969. He had made his debut in 1965 under Casey Stengel. Ron and I have stayed in contact periodically. In fact, Sheridan and I stayed with Ron and his wife, Cecilia, in their home in New Orleans on our way to Mets fantasy camp in 2009. We had a good time with the Swobodas. They are very good people and we enjoyed them tremendously. He's been a broadcaster down there for a few decades. Ron can still get fired up. Just ask Jim Mora, the Saints coach, who had a spirited interview with Ron one time.

Best friends Cleon Jones and Tommie Agee played left and center field. They grew up in Mobile, Alabama. I used to hang around them once in awhile and they could really play the game. Agee was Rookie of the Year with the White Sox and came over to the Mets in 1968. He was beaned by Bob Gibson in spring training and didn't have a good year in 1968 but he rebounded big time in '69. He could be my pick as MVP of the team that year. Even though Cleon hit .340 and Seaver had a Cy Young year, Agee did a great job out of the leadoff spot and hit 26 homers. And that was coming off a year in which he hit .217 with five home runs. Cleon could hit and play the outfield. The two of them were excellent football players, also.

Art Shamsky is the one 1969 Met that I have been in contact with through all these years. He is a wonderful and very caring individual, and always treated me super. If it wasn't for him, I wouldn't have made the team, not that I wanted him or anybody to get hurt, but that's how I got my opportunity and I took advantage of it. Maybe it's because of that World Series that a lot of us stay in touch with each other. Art and I talk to each other at least once a month, and I see him when he comes out to California for business. As you know, we had a very close team and I stay in touch with a number of the guys, but Shamsky is the guy I'm in contact with the most. He is probably my favorite 1969 Met.

 The team was made up of good guys. They didn't hammer. Once you proved you could play a little bit, they respected you. There was no hazing the new guy. They didn't call me "Rook."

On May 6, we beat the Reds 8-1. Jim Maloney had thrown threw a few no-hitters in his career, but I led off the game with a double against him. The next night I was hitless in four at-bats against Jim Merritt and Clay Carroll. I later played Triple-A ball with Merritt in Indianapolis. We called him Badge, like a merit badge. Merritt pitched seven shutout innings against us that night. That was May 7, and I wasn't in the starting lineup again until May 25. I was hitting .212, maybe that's why, you think?

Over the next two and a half weeks, if I played, it was as a pinch-hitter or pinch-runner. On the 16th in Cincinnati, I broke a 6-6 tie with a two-run single in the seventh off George Culver. I had a few moments of glory in hitting. But then I didn't play in the next two games, and my next appearance was as a pinch-hitter in the ninth inning of a 15-3 loss in Atlanta. I'm not making excuses, but unless you're playing every day, it's hard to get into a groove. I think that's true for most ballplayers. And I was used to playing every day.

We were 18-18 after a win at Atlanta, but then we lost five in a row, including a three-game sweep in Houston. We couldn't win at the Astrodome that year. That's the only team we couldn't beat. We went 2-10 against them, and lost the last nine meetings. We had a winning record against every other team in the league except Cincinnati, who we went .500 against. The Astrodome was a big park. It was new and everybody was enthralled with it but it wasn't a good place for the New York Mets to play. Looking at our record, obviously we didn't like it there. The year before, the Astros beat the Mets 1-0 in a 24-inning game, with Al Weis making an error to end the game. I started the final game of the sweep in Houston, going 1-4 with a double in the ninth.

My next appearance was as a pinch-hitter in a 3-2 loss to the Padres. I grounded out against Al Santorini. We had lost five in a row at that point and were 18-23. I don't believe there was any panic on our team, but of course there were negative people who probably thought the Mets were done for the year. They're going to fold just like in their past history…same-old Mets. I don't think so. You go on a five-game losing streak, sure you're going to have people saying that this is the end of the Mets, and it's nice they did well for a month. That's human nature to think that the team would continue losing. But then we won 11 in a row. Gil was later asked when he thought the Mets were for real, he pointed to that winning streak. He thought that was the turning point for us.

May 30: Home Run

I had been out the night before and I got home early in the morning. I didn't really sleep all night and didn't expect to play. When I knew I was going to play I took care of myself the night before. I went to the ballpark and saw that I'm hitting second in the lineup and I'm really ticked off. We were playing against the Giants and Mike McCormick, a left-handed pitcher who had won the Cy Young in 1967. We were down 3-1 with two outs in the eighth and I hit a home run into the bullpen in leftfield. The crowd at Shea was so loud. That started a two-out rally and we took a 4-3 lead and held on to win.

It's funny that the only home run of my major league career came after a long night out. Max McGee, the great Packers receiver, once said "When it's third and 10, you can take the milk drinkers. I'll take the whiskey drinkers every time." I wasn't out drinking whiskey, because I hardly drank at all. But I know what he meant. He was a guy who was out the night before the first Super Bowl thinking that he wasn't going to play, and then caught a few touchdown passes after another Green Bay player got injured.

After the win against the Giants, I was on Kiner's Korner. Ralph, Bob Murphy and Lindsey Nelson were super guys. I wish I had the tape of my appearance but most of those shows have been taped over through the years by the network. That was my only time on the show. It came at a good time. We all had our clutch moments when we won ballgames. We spread it around pretty good. I played with McCormick a few years later in Hawaii and he never brought the home run up. I don't even know if he remembered that I hit a home run off him.

Like I said, we hit .242 as a team, and had to win a lot of 1-0, 2-1 games. But we got clutch hits. I had a few clutch hits and knocked in important runs. We all did.

55

The next day I was back on the bench and pinch-hit against Ron Herbel, who I was traded for at the end of the 1970 season. I grounded out but we won the game.

Mets record at the end of May:
21-23, 9 games out of first

June 1969

We began June with a 5-4 win against the Giants, even though I didn't play. Then the Dodgers came to town. I had a hit off Claude Osteen but I was out stretching it into a double. In the ninth, with Koosman holding on to a 2-1 lead, Wes Parker doubled to right and I made a throwing error allowing him to take third with nobody out. But then Koosman got Andy Kosco and Bill Sudakis on pop-ups and Jim Lefebvre flew out to left. Jerry sure bailed me out. Everybody bailed out everybody that year. That was only his second win of the season and he still ended up winning 17. And that game was two hours and one minute. Isn't that great? I love it.

After that win we were back at .500. The next day I was on the bench, although I don't think it was because of the error. Gil knew me better than that. He knew I was a good outfielder. We won 5-2 and had a winning record again. Then we completed the sweep with a 1-0 win in 15 innings. Bill Singer and Jack DiLauro both pitched nine innings of two-hit shutout ball. And that was DiLauro's first career start. McGraw pitched four shutout innings and then Ron Taylor came on to pitch. I entered in the 14th inning in a double-switch. Unlike pinch-hitting, it wasn't tough for me to come in as a defensive replacement. As long as it wasn't too cold. The weather in June was OK with me. I flew out to center against Al McBean to end the 14th. We won it when Tommie Agee scored on a Garrett hit to center which Willie Davis misplayed. Davis was very talented but he didn't seem to work hard at his profession.

Then we had our first West Coast road trip. We went to play the Padres in San Diego at Jack Murphy Stadium. They had a huge ballpark. It was 420 feet to centerfield. I started the first game against Johnny Podres and went three-for-three with two sacrifices and an RBI triple in the ninth off Jack Baldschun as we won 4-1. Podres had been the hero of the 1955 World Series for the Dodgers, and was in his final season in the majors. That was one of my better games. And then the next day I was back on the bench. I was probably thinking that I would play the next game but oh well, that's how it goes. Shamsky was in right. I pinch-hit for Seaver late and we came back to win it for him. The Padres played us well that year.

Next we went to Candlestick Park. It was terribly cold and the fans were awful. We won the first game of the series 9-4, our eleventh win in a row. It was a different lineup than usual. I was in right field, Swoboda was in left and Cleon was at first against Mike McCormick. I had one hit in five at-bats and scored a run. They had a good team. They really had some bombers with Mays, McCovey, and Bobby Bonds. Plus they had Juan Marichal, Gaylord Perry's spitter and Ray Sadecki. I never had contact with Mays. I never talked to the opposing team anyway. Funny thing is I don't remember Mays doing a lot against us, but McCovey did. He hammered us in a lot of games.

San Francisco was a nice city. We got fined in Chicago once because somebody had a party. We had midnight curfews because of the day games in Chicago. Most guys were at this party. Not everybody like Seaver or guys who knew better. We were at the Executive House in Chicago. So we get back after curfew and Gil is sitting and waiting for us in the lobby. He got about 15 of us...one hundred bucks a pop. Back when they fined the ballplayers. That was a lot of money for us. That was rare for me because I didn't really carouse that much. And we weren't a wild bunch. We had some beer drinkers but nobody who drank excessively, and we weren't drug users. Knowing Hodges, he probably knew about the party. He had his ways of finding things out. That's what a manager's job is.

The role of the manager was a little different back then. We didn't have all the scouting reports like they have now. There was really nothing written down. I don't remember any pregame meetings for strategy purposes. The meetings were mainly for pitchers and catchers to discuss how to go after hitters. As a former position player, Hodges didn't really have many meetings with the whole team. If he wanted something done, he could send a coach to talk to us. And if it was really important, he would talk one-on-one, but there was no big meeting necessary. He would bring you into his office, but he would never embarrass you in front of the team. During the game, they would position us from the dugout if we weren't in the correct position for a hitter.

I was out of the lineup when the winning streak was snapped in a 7-2 loss. Then we went to Los Angeles for three games against the Dodgers. They had a nice stadium. It was still new at the time, and now it's one of the oldest in the league. It hasn't changed much. My parents came from Hawaii to see me play.

When we were out in San Francisco, my dad flew on the charter flight with us to Los Angeles and ended up sitting next to Casey Stengel. My dad was so excited meeting Casey and shaking his hand that he said he didn't wash his hand for a week. Normally it was just players traveling, no wives or other family. There were exceptions, so I asked Gil if my dad could fly with us and he said no problem. I'm glad he got the chance to do that.

While we were in Los Angeles, I rented a car and drove to Long Beach with Gary Gentry. So I'm on the 405 Freeway during the day, because the Dodgers had night games, and it was packed. So what I did, because I was real hyper, I went on the side area of the freeway, in the non-lane areas, and I zipped past all the traffic that had stopped. Too bad that was illegal, and a cop stopped me and gave me a ticket. I probably could have been thrown in jail, so I was fine to settle for the ticket for illegally driving on a freeway. But we did get back to Dodger Stadium in time for the game that night.

We lost the first game 1-0 with me on the bench. Then Seaver beat Don Sutton the next day with me sitting again. In the final game of the series, Don Drysdale started for the Dodgers. I pinch-hit in the ninth and grounded out against Jim Brewer in a 3-2 loss. Billy Martin once punched Brewer during a fight. Billy hit a few guys. During the 1969 season while managing Minnesota, Billy hit Dave Boswell, and Dave was one of his pitchers!

The day the series ended was also the day we traded for Donn Clendenon. Donn was very outgoing. He was an attorney. He was very aggressive and competitive. Donn would stir the pot, get on guys, and get guys fired up. He was a big addition when we got him on June 15. He added a lot of power to the club and ended up as the World Series MVP. He had quite a personality. I will put it this way. You knew when Clendenon was around.

When we traded for him, I didn't know much about his background. I found out later that he was quite a hitter with Pittsburgh when they had Stargell, Clemente, and all the guys over there. Obviously, the Mets knew what they were doing when they traded for him. The Mets traded some very good prospects to get him including Steve Renko. Renko had once been the quarterback at Kansas when Gale Sayers was in the backfield. Donn wasn't happy early in the season and there had been a failed trade to Houston and we got him from the Expos. Donn could really hit in the clutch.

We split a doubleheader in Philadelphia. I entered the first game as a defensive replacement in the ninth inning as we won 1-0. In the second game, I grounded out against Grant Jackson in a 7-3 loss. Jackson was an All-Star in 1969, and later pitched in the World Series with the Orioles, Yankees and Pirates. The next day, Koosman beat them 2-0, and again I entered the game for defense in the ninth.

On June 19, I entered the game as a defensive replacement in the eighth inning. In the top of the ninth, Ken Boswell singled in two runs with two outs to put us up 6-5. I grounded out to end the inning. Then I was replaced in right by Swoboda, which is funny that I would be replaced one inning after going into the game. We held on for the win.

Back at Shea Stadium, Nolan Ryan beat Bob Gibson in the first game of our series with St. Louis. We were up 4-2 and Gibson hit for himself leading off the seventh inning. He homered off Tug. I entered in the eighth inning for defense and we won 4-3. The next day we lost 5-3. I pinch-hit against Nelson Briles, walked and scored a run. I never thought that guy had good stuff but he would win. He won titles with the Cardinals and Pirates. I never was impressed with him but he probably wasn't very impressed with me either.

Then we had a doubleheader against the Cardinals. We beat Steve Carlton in the first game although I didn't play. In the second game, we led 1-0 in the top of the eighth. The Cardinals had two runners on and one out. Joe Torre came up and Lou Brock was on second base. Torre singled and Brock tried to score but I threw him out from left field. I guess he was trying to run on the rookie. Maybe he didn't get as good a lead with one out as he would have with two outs. We held on to win with Koosman beating Mike Torrez.

Next was another doubleheader, this one against the Phillies. Both games were under two hours. This was when Richie Allen went to the race track and got stuck in traffic and couldn't play against us. He worked in the horse racing business later on. I ended up playing with his two brothers. Ronnie, his younger brother, was a teammate of mine in Tidewater in 1970, and I later played with Hank Allen in Hawaii. Richie was a very nice guy. I remember being on first base once and he'd be talking. The fans were tough on him in Philadelphia, always yelling at him and booing him. He would write on the infield dirt "Boo" with his foot. He was suspended for awhile after missing the doubleheader. The Phillies traded him after the season even though he led the team in home runs. I didn't play in the first game but had a single and walk in the nightcap. Jim McAndrew only allowed two singles. There were no balls hit to me in left field. There were a lot of ground balls against McAndrew.

We led the Phillies 5-0 the next day but trailed 6-5 heading into the bottom of the 10th. With two outs and a runner on, they intentionally walked Cleon, the winning run, to get to me. That's a big-time insult. Then Bill Wilson unintentionally walked me to load the bases but Ed Kranepool grounded out. The Phillies beat us again the following day with me pinch-hitting against Grant Jackson and lining out to third.

Then on to Pittsburgh, where I struck out looking against Joe Gibbon in the ninth inning with the tying runs on base. After sitting the next day, I went 0-for-5 against Bob Veale, Bruce Dal Canton and Chuck Hartenstein. Now here's something different. After the three-for-three game I had in San Diego, I didn't play the next day but after the oh-for-five, Gil stuck with me and had me in the starting lineup the next day. Go figure that one. I had a two-run single off Nelson Briles in the first inning, and I doubled off Ray Washburn. Washburn had pitched a no-hitter the year before against the Giants. We won 10-2 in St. Louis although again there were no balls hit to me with McAndrew on the mound.

Mets record at the end of June:
40-32, 7.5 games out of first

July 1969

We began the month in St. Louis with a doubleheader. I had a hit off Steve Carlton, who I hit pretty well, and started a 9-6-3 double play. I went 0-for-5 in the second game against Mike Torrez and Joe Hoerner as we lost both games. Some guys didn't care for doubleheaders but I liked them because I wanted to play all the time. In my case I wanted to play as much as I could because I wasn't playing that much at the time. Normally we prefer one game a day, especially in the summertime when it gets hot. But I didn't mind. I just liked playing the game.

Busch Stadium was nice but it was hotter than blazes during the summer. It was a new stadium, having opened in 1966. They had artificial turf on the field and it was smoking. It would get to be 110 degrees on the field. When you're young, you don't pay as much attention to it. I preferred grass fields but the turf didn't bother me any. I didn't have any leg issues on turf even though some guys did. Not me though. I was able to stay healthy during my professional career. It amazes me about how often these kids are on the Disabled List now. What a joke. I don't get it. You would think with today's modern medicine and modern rehabilitation you wouldn't think they'd have all these issues. Maybe it's too much weight lifting. We didn't want to be on the disabled list because we were afraid somebody would take our job. I know I didn't. I wouldn't tell anyone if I was hurt or anything. I was in good shape and sturdy.

After taking the next two in St. Louis, we went to Pittsburgh for a July 4 doubleheader. I was hitless in five at-bats but we won both games. Then I had a hit, walk, and run on July 6.

The Cubs came to Shea for three games. It was exciting with them in first place and we were in contention, so every game we played against them was a big deal. And we had exciting games against them. In the opener, Kranepool had the game-winning hit to left. Ferguson Jenkins stayed in the whole game as we rallied for three runs in the ninth.

In that ninth inning there was a double that Clendenon hit that Don Young didn't catch in center. Leo Durocher and Ron Santo publicly got all over Young for that, which is terrible. You should never do that. If I had made a mistake like that, Gil or Clendenon would let me know in private, not yell to the guys in the press. Especially Hodges, he would never do that. But Durocher was not the smartest guy in the world. He talked quite a bit. He put his foot in his mouth, especially when he said things about us. It's too bad they hammered that guy like that. The thing is, they were right. The ball should've been caught. Ken Boswell had also reached on a double to start the inning that Young went back on and then the ball fell in front of him. Nowadays, a runner would be on first if that happened.

The next night, Tom Seaver almost pitched a perfect game. Jimmy Qualls singled with one out in the ninth on a ball to left-center out of the reach of Agee. Qualls was playing instead of Don Young. I played right field for the last two innings. We were hoping he'd finish it off. You're always a little on edge when a guy has a perfect game going because you don't want to mess it up. He was just two outs away. Clendenon went over to him to get him to refocus and get the last two outs, which he did.

I've always wondered in my mind, if I was in centerfield, because my glove was on my right hand and the ball was hit to left-center, whereas Tommie's glove was on his left hand, I wonder if I would've had a shot at it. But I've seen the replay before and it would've been an awful tough play for anybody to get to the ball because it was quite a ways away from him. Having looked at the replay again, it was hit in the right spot, that's for sure. I would've loved to have had an attempt at the ball. I always got good jumps on the ball so I wonder if I could've made the play. I still wonder to this day. But we'll never know, will we?

Chicago took the final game from us. Leo Durocher said those were the real Mets on the field. He opened his big mouth. They still didn't believe we could do it. Nobody did, not just him. I don't care what sport you're playing, you can't take games for granted against anybody. Obviously we proved people wrong. Maybe it's because I was a rookie, but it didn't bother me who we were playing. I thought we could beat anybody. I just thought about our team and what we could do and what we had accomplished up to that point.

Before facing the Cubs again, we had three games against the Expos. We lost the first 11-4. I pinch-hit and popped up to short against Dick Radatz, The Monster, a former All-Star. Then we took both games of a doubleheader and I was a defensive replacement in the ninth inning of each game.

Then we played the Cubs again, this time at Wrigley Field. Bill Hands beat us 1-0 with me on the bench. Ron Santo was clicking his heels after Cubs wins at that point. He was a hot dog. He started doing it and Swoboda made some comments about it. We won the next game with Al Weis hitting a three-run homer. It was his first homer of the year and he was playing at short because Bud Harrelson was in the Army reserves. And then we won the next day with Al hitting another home run. Those were his only two of the regular season. He was a clutch ballplayer. Hodges loved him. He could play anywhere in the infield. He was always clutch. Al was a good ballplayer. We had taken four of six from the Cubs. We were legit. There was no doubt about that.

After that series, we went to Montreal. We split the first two games and then had a doubleheader on July 20. We lost the first game 3-2. The second game was tied in the 10th with a runner on third and two outs when Bobby Pfeil bunted for a single. Two outs, man on third. I think it's a great time to bunt because the third baseman is usually playing back and Bob laid down a perfect bunt. Bobby was always a very heads-up player, very smart and knew how to play the game. He was called up in the summer and played 40 games at third. Bobby was another good guy and one that I still stay in contact with. I talk to him every other month. He was one of my better buddies on that 1969 team. He's in Stockton, California, now. He's in the apartment building business and he's done very well for himself. I can see why, as he is such a sharp guy.

I watched the moon landing with the rest of the Mets in the bar area of the Montreal airport. The joke was that man would walk on the moon before the Mets won the pennant. Well, they beat us by a few months.

We lost our next game to the Reds in 12 innings. I had a bunt single off Jim Merritt, my future teammate in Indianapolis. The next day I flew out as a pinch-hitter against Jim Maloney, who pitched a few no-hitters in his time, but we won the game.

On July 26, Seaver was leading 3-2 and Gil put me in right field in the ninth. With Bobby Tolan on first, I caught a Tony Perez line drive and threw to first for a double play. They have coaches on first and third who always to say to hold on a line drive but it happens. I can't think for Tolan but you see the ball hit hard and you think that's going to be a base hit, but that's not necessarily true. Cincinnati beat us the next day with Gerry Arigio pitching into the eighth inning. I pinch-hit in the sixth and got three at-bats in four innings, going two-for-three and reaching on an error.

July 30: Astros Doubleheader

Houston blew us out 16-3 in the first game and was pounding us in game two when Cleon didn't run full out on what turned out to be a double by one of the Astros. Gil walks out and everybody thinks he's going to the pitcher's mound. He bypasses the mound, and Harrelson is playing short and Bud is thinking Uh-oh, what did I do? He was scared that Gil was walking toward him. Then he bypasses Harrelson and goes into the outfield and says, "OK, Cleon, let's go." There are mixed stories about if Cleon was hurt. I don't know. All I know is that Cleon didn't play for a few days.

That was another indication that you don't mess with Gil Hodges. We knew who the boss was and to this day I know that Cleon respects Gil. It was a big statement to take him out in front of all those people. After the game, Gil told the media that Cleon was hurt. He didn't get on Cleon or anything. He wouldn't do that.

In my history in baseball, I had never seen a manager take a player out like that. But the 1969 Amazin' Mets gave people a lot of things that people hadn't seen before.

I didn't play in either game of the doubleheader in which we were outscored 27-8. I'm sure that's why we lost. Gil should've started me. Joking aside, I did play the next day and had two hits in a 2-0 loss where we only managed four hits. I almost threw out a runner at home but Grote was charged with an error for dropping the ball. Shame on him. He normally didn't drop balls. Houston killed us. Some teams just beat up on you. They had some really good pitchers. Tom Griffin, who started the last game of the series, had the best slider I had ever seen in my life. He was a rookie that year and went on to pitch 14 seasons in the majors. They also had Larry Dierker and Don Wilson, two All-Star pitchers. They had some guys that could throw the ball.

Mets record at the end of July:
55-44, 6.5 games out of first

August 1969

I had a two-run single off Phil Niekro in a 5-4 win over the Braves to open the month. Cleon Jones always said that hitting against Niekro put him in a slump. It's hard to hit that knuckleball. There's nothing you can do to prepare for it. You just have to go up there and wait for it. He also struck me out twice in that game.

Then we beat Atlanta 1-0. In the seventh, I bunted Swoboda over to second and he came in to score the only run. We all contributed. We all got key hits. We hit in the clutch, that's for sure, because we didn't score a bunch of runs. And I was a good bunter. I always worked on bunting. We all did. Seaver was a good bunter. Nobody seems to learn how to bunt anymore. I don't get that at all. And only certain guys bunt. We could all bunt. Heck, I learned when I was a little kid how to bunt. You've got to get the guy over any way you can.

We finished a sweep of Atlanta, coming from five runs down. I doubled off Felipe Alou at first base in the first inning on a 9-3 double play. I had a couple of those that year. In the sixth, we were down 5-1 and I bunted for a single to load the bases. It's a good time to bunt, one out, push bunt trying to bunt for a hit. We tied the game and Grote won it with a home run. Like Weis, he didn't hit a lot, but he hit them when they counted.

The Reds beat us in a few games in Cincinnati. Jim Maloney beat us 1-0 and then they beat Seaver, who dropped to 15-7. That was his last loss until the World Series. The Reds played us tough and went .500 against us that year. They were one year away from the World Series themselves. We won the next game 10-1, with me pinch-running for Cleon and going 0-for-2 against Jack Fisher.

We split a doubleheader in Atlanta. In game one, I pinch-ran for Cleon and scored a run in a 4-1 win. I was leading off and playing leftfield in the second game. I threw out Orlando Cepeda trying to go to second on a hit. Those guys will never learn, will they? But we lost 1-0 in 10 innings. The game was 2 hours and 11 minutes, which isn't bad for 10 innings. Their pitcher was Ron Reed, a big, tall, right-hander, who went all 10 innings. I was 1-4. There was an Old-Timers' game in the early '90s at Shea where they had the '69 Mets against some other players and I doubled to left against Reed to score a run. But he shut us out that day. He was a pretty good basketball player too.

That 1-0 loss on August 8 was the last time I was in the starting lineup until September. I was a pinch-hitter and stayed in to play right field in the next two wins against the Braves. Then we went to Houston and they smoked us again. Tom Griffin beat us in the opener, and I grounded out as a pinch-hitter in the seventh. Koosman blew a 5-1 lead the next day. Gil sent me up as a pinch-hitter down 8-7 with two on and two outs in the ninth. I could've been a hero but I hit a fly ball to center. He had me pinch-hit for Al Weis, who was a clutch hitter, but I was batting left-handed. Gil's lineups were always that way. He liked those lefty-righty matchups and did a lot of platooning.

Then the Astros completed the sweep the next day. We couldn't beat Houston. We lost 10 out of 12 games against the Astros, so we were glad to be done with them. They were the only club we couldn't beat. They kicked our butts. We lost all six games at the Astrodome.

After August 13, were 62-51, 10 games behind the Cubs, with the Cardinals in second. But I don't remember us ever being down mentally. Even when we were 10 games out. I think one of the things is that we were so young, it didn't bother us any. Maybe some teams, it would've bothered them. With a manager like Hodges, he wouldn't let us get down. I don't remember anybody being down. We always thought we could win.

Then San Diego came to town and we took off. At least the pitching took off. We scored a combined 11 runs in the next five games and won all five. That's pretty good pitching. We swept the Padres in two doubleheaders. I was a defensive replacement in the ninth inning of three games.

San Francisco was next. Tommie Agee hit a home-run to end the game in the 14th against Marichal, who went the distance. He wouldn't come out. How many kids are going to throw nine innings nowadays, let alone 14? Gary Gentry pitched 10 innings and Tug pitched the final four. I came in for defense in the 11th and Marichal struck me out looking in the bottom of the inning. That's usually how I struck out. I didn't swing and miss a lot. He was basically challenging the rookie with fastballs down the middle and I couldn't hit them. And he got me out before Agee's homer.

We split the next two against the Giants. I appeared as a defensive replacement and pinch-runner. Then we took three in a row from the Dodgers. Grote won the middle game with a double in the ninth. Next we went to San Diego and won three straight. I didn't play in two of the games and entered one late for defense. I was playing less but it never really bothered me because I was just happy that we were winning. Again, you want to play, but if you're not playing and you're winning, it's OK.

After that sweep, we were 2.5 games behind Chicago. We had erased 7.5 games off the lead in two weeks. The Cubs had an older team and I think they were getting a little tired. Marichal ended the winning streak with a 5-0 win against us at Candlestick Park.

August 30: The Throw: 7-2-3-5 Double Play

Tug McGraw was pitching in a tie game in the ninth, and the winning run was on first for the Giants. Willie McCovey was at the plate with one out and Gil decided not to intentionally walk him. There was a shift, so I was the left fielder playing towards centerfield, Agee was in right-center and Swoboda was down the right-field line. Tug threw a screwball and McCovey reached out and hit one down the left-field line. As soon as he hit it, I just took off knowing that the winning run was going to score unless I could do something.

I sprinted to the ball, picked it up about a foot away from the line, pivoted, took a hop, and fired. Watch an outfielder make a throw nowadays. A lot of them take three, four, five steps to get rid of the ball. I could get rid of it in less than a step and a half, and in that case I didn't even take any steps. The momentum from pivoting gave me power to throw the ball a long way. Whitey Herzog had taught me how to do that a few years before.

I fired a strike to Grote at home to get Bob Burda. Grote, thinking there were three outs, rolled the ball to the mound and McCovey kept running. Clendenon, being the heads-up player that he was, picked it up and threw to Bobby Pfeil at third to get McCovey. The next inning, Clendenon hit the game-winning home run.

That was typical of our games. We won a lot of games in dramatic fashion. We weren't going to beat ourselves. We knew how to play the game. Gil knew what buttons to push. We were the best team in baseball and one of the best of all time, and I think most of my teammates would agree.

Between the home run and this throw, I was becoming the Giant slayer. It amazed me that I could throw the ball on a line that far. People talk about Bo Jackson's arm, and he had a better arm than I did, but the throw I made was on a line. Some of these guys' throws are more in the air. Yasiel Puig had a highlight throw in Colorado and that one was a rainbow. I threw mine from right in front of the warning track over 300 feet, shoulder high to Grote. It was a blind throw. I just pivoted and fired in the direction of Grote. It surprised him because he made the tag and thought there were three outs.

I guess I'm tooting my own horn. To be realistic, I'd put my defense up against anybody who ever played the outfield, even though I didn't play that long. I hate to sound like I'm bragging, but it's a fact. Mickey Mantle could go get them, but he didn't have the arm. Willie Mays was probably the best of all. I loved throwing somebody out. To me, it was better than getting a big hit. People sometimes ask me if I would rather get a big hit or throw somebody out, and I say throw somebody out. I didn't do one thing well, I did three or four well. That's why I played professional baseball for 10 years.

I had entered that game in the eighth inning. There was nowhere to throw during the game either. I just threw back and forth with Agee before the innings began. I must've been loose because I threw a rocket to Grote.

74

I threw a lot during that season. Every third or fourth day at Shea Stadium, I'd throw the ball from left-center to the ball boy in the right-field corner. My arm was in great shape, the best it had ever been in. Every so often, I'd let one fly and purposely throw it into the stands because people were behind the ball boy down the right field line, hoping I would throw it in the stands. But I'd go out before a game, usually when I wasn't starting, and do that long-toss for about 20 minutes. It was just to keep my arm strong because I knew what my job was, especially at the end of the season, was going to be as a defensive replacement in a lot of games, so I had to keep that arm strong. I never had a sore arm. Obviously it paid off. When I fielded that ball McCovey hit, I was ready to go. Plus, running from the gap to the line got my adrenaline going. You don't think about it, you just fire it. And I threw it on a line.

A few years ago I saw Grote at a minor-league game in Texas. He brought that up. He said, "That throw you threw me, it shocked the heck out of me. I couldn't believe you threw that ball from the left-field corner like that on a line." He said it kind of stunned him. And Jerry was always a heads-up player.

The month ended with us splitting a doubleheader. In game one, I pinch-hit for Cleon in the fifth and had two hits off Bobby Bolin. Don McMahon got me out in that game. He pitched until he was 44. Those were our last games against the Giants, who actually finished August in first place in the West.

**Mets record at the end of August:
76-54, 4.5 games out of first**

September 1969

On September 8, the Cubs would come to Shea Stadium for a pair of games, but we still had a week of games to play first. You can't look too far ahead. Yeah, it's exciting to think about an upcoming series with a contending club. But I didn't get too fired up. They were just somebody else we had to beat, like all the other teams we played.

We lost two out of three at Dodger Stadium to open the month, with me only playing two innings in left field. Koosman lost the first game and didn't make it out of the first, so Gil brought him back as the starter two days later. If he only pitched one inning, why not? But again, it was a different era. That first start was like the equivalent of throwing a bullpen in between starts. If it was now, they would just have specialists pitch from the fifth or sixth inning on.

Back at Shea Stadium, I was in the starting lineup for the first time in nearly a month as we took game one of a doubleheader against the Phillies. Seaver won his 20th game, and I had a hit, walked, and scored a run. The game was one hour and 58 minutes. Tom threw strikes. It's too bad they didn't keep pitch counts to look back at. We also took the next three from the Phillies, and I singled in two runs off John Boozer in the last game.

We were 2.5 games behind Chicago when the Cubs came to town for a two-game series. They could leave 4.5 up or we could cut the lead to a half game.

Cubs manager Leo Durocher wasn't the most well-liked guy. He went way back to Babe Ruth's days. He even ticked Babe off when they were teammates. Durocher ticked everybody off. He was just a mouthy guy that just didn't know when to shut up, but obviously he did something right because people kept hiring him. He ran the Cubs into the ground though. They had an older team. You look at our rosters, we could field a team of nine guys under 24. They had older guys and Leo started them in every game, and then later in the year, when it gets hot in Chicago, he just wore those older guys out. And Gil just platooned us quite a bit so were always fresh, plus we were younger. It makes a difference.

On paper, if you look at the 1969 Cubs and 1969 Mets, it's no comparison. They had some big-name players and you look at the Mets and go, Who are these guys? We didn't have the names as far as position players were concerned. They had Ernie Banks, Ron Santo, Billy Williams. And they had Ferguson Jenkins on the mound. They had some horses out there.

Bill Hands nearly beaned Agee at the start of the first game. Then Koosman drilled Ron Santo. And as a teammate, you love it. He would do that. You don't mess with Koosman. Or Seaver. Or Ryan. Or Gentry. But especially Koosman. And then the next time up, Agee hit a bomb off of Hands. Later in the game, Agee scored on a Wayne Garrett single on a close play at the plate to give us the lead. Randy Hundley and Leo Durocher were both arguing about that one. That's a hard call. I watched the replay online. He slid over Hundley's left leg. Hundley was fortunate that Agee didn't slide into his leg because he would've broken his leg. Hundley's left leg was over the line in front of home plate. If he slid into his leg he would've broken it, no doubt, with as hard as Tommie ran. Hundley got him on the backside with the tag but the umpire said nope. Koosman struck out 13 and held on to win 3-2.

77

The next night, a black cat ran in front of the Cubs dugout and stared at Durocher. They never did find the cat. And nobody knows where it came from. Seaver pitched and won 7-1. He almost hit a home run off Jenkins and had to settle for a double. Tom made himself a good hitter. He worked hard at hitting, and he worked hard at pitching. He worked hard at everything. There's a clip of Tom showing him sliding headfirst into second base. He wasn't just a great pitcher. He worked on all facets of his game. He knew it would help him win ballgames and help the team win ballgames. How many pitchers do that? Work on all areas of the game. Base running, bunting and hitting for a starting pitcher. He was a smart guy and knew what he had to do. And he wasn't bad on the mound. Reggie Jackson once said that blind people go to the ballpark just to hear Seaver pitch.

Then on September 10, we went into first place.

We had a two-night doubleheader against the Expos. In game one, I entered as a pinch-runner in the eighth and stayed in right field. Another example of how things change: tie game, bottom of the ninth, winning run on first with two outs and Gil let Jim McAndrew hit for himself. He struck out but pitched two more innings. In the 12th, I came up with Cleon on first and two outs and walked on four pitches against Bill Stoneman. Then Boswell singled to center to score Cleon. We moved ahead of the Cubs by percentage points.

It wasn't tough for me to draw that walk as opposed to trying to hit one into the gap. Just another way the game has changed. I was watching a game the other day that was tied. There was a tie game in the ninth inning and as a leadoff guy, your job is to get on. But this guy was swinging at pitches ahead in the count and out of the strike zone. Take a strike. You would think the manager would tell his guys to take one.

78

It just doesn't make sense. We had a different way of playing the game. That's why I think we would beat these guys now. There's no doubt in my mind we would win games like that. We would do the little things it takes to win the games. We would take walks unless it was a power hitter like Clendenon. That's how I was raised in the game, to get on base and to score, no matter how you get on. Whether it's a hit, a walk, or an error, who cares? I drew a lot of walks, especially in the minor leagues. I knew what my job was. I don't think a lot of guys now know what their job is. If you're a leadoff hitter, your job is to get on base and let the big boys knock you in. they don't think that way anymore. They all want to hit the home run. And the management seems to go for it. Go figure.

But I digress. After moving intto first, we had to play another game that night. Obviously it didn't bother us because we won the next game. It helps when Nolan Ryan pitches a complete game three-hitter. The next day, I had an RBI single in the eighth inning as Gentry beat the Expos 4-0.

Then we went to Pittsburgh and swept a doubleheader. We won both games 1-0 with Koosman and Cardwell knocking in the run in each game. That's a classic Mets game. Our starting pitcher in each game knocked in the only run. To me, that symbolizes the New York Mets from 1969. We won another classic a few days later in St. Louis. We struck out 19 times against Steve Carlton but still won 4-3 on two two-run homers from Ron Swoboda. Those things don't happen. How can he get 19 strikeouts and lose?

It just shows you, every game a different guy would win it. Garrett with the hit against the Cubs, Boswell with his hit, Koosman and Cardwell in the 1-0 games, Swoboda with the home runs. There's always somebody doing something. It wasn't always Cleon or Clendenon, it was everybody. Bobby

Pfeil with his bunt single against the Expos in July. Al Weis with his home runs in consecutive games against the Cubs. That's what made us such a great team. I don't know if there's ever been a season like that, but it was incredible.

I didn't play from the 12th to the 18th. We went 6-1 so Gil didn't need to play me. We lost in both ends of a doubleheader to the Pirates on the 19th. I was a pinch-hitter in both games.

We were on the wrong side of a memorable game on September 20 when Bob Moose no-hit us at Shea Stadium. I pinch-hit in the ninth inning and drew a leadoff walk. I was on second when Art Shamsky grounded out to end it. I got off the field quickly. Who wants to be on the field when the other team beat you? I didn't want to watch them celebrate
.

We swept a doubleheader the next day. In game two, I led off and played centerfield. It was my first start in over two weeks and I doubled and scored in the first inning. I walked in the fourth but Steve Blass picked me off. He got me and he was a righty. He had a good move. I'm sure Gil didn't like that. He'd just look at you. He didn't say anything. He didn't have to say anything. He'd just give you that look. He didn't like those mental mistakes, I'll tell you that. But what manager does? We didn't make too many of them.

The Cardinals came to Queens for our last home series of the season. Seaver won the first game. Then we won the next night in 11 innings. I had entered the game in the 11th and Bud Harrelson drove in the winning run with a single off Bob Gibson, who was still on the mound.

We had a chance to clinch the division in our last home game of the year. It's always great winning at home. You want to clinch everything at home. Plus the Cubs hadn't been eliminated yet and we had to end the season with two games at Wrigley, so it would be nice to make sure we wrapped it up by then. Gentry was the losing pitcher in the Moose no-hitter but he pitched a complete game shutout against the Cardinals. We hit a few home runs off Steve Carlton early and Gentry did the rest. We celebrated pretty good. We were just young kids celebrating, having a good time, not even concerned that we had beaten the two-time defending NL champion Cardinals.

Then we went to Philadelphia and swept three straight, not even allowing a run. Our staff had a string of 42 straight shutout innings. I led off the first game of the series and went hitless in five at-bats. For the final few games of the season, Cleon led off because he was going for the batting title and Gil was trying to get him as many at-bats as possible.

Before going to Chicago to end the season, we went back to Shea to play in the Mayor's Trophy Game against the Yankees. We were supposed to play it in July before the Cubs came to town but it was rained out. The Yankees had a lefty, Steve Hamilton, and he threw a blooper pitch. It was called a Folly Floater. I hit against him and I was trying to hit that sucker and I popped it up but we were laughing while we were playing and he threw that pitch to me. Too bad we didn't play that game at Yankee Stadium, because that would've been my one chance to go there. It would've been an incredible experience to play at the original Stadium and being out there when they still had the monuments in the outfield. I kick myself for not going over there and seeing that ballpark during that year. I should have made a point of going there, but like a dummy, I didn't. Although I suppose it would've been weird for a Met to use his day off to see Yankee Stadium. I could've gone there but I didn't think about those things at the time. It was no big deal to me.

We were off the next day and then played in Chicago. It's kind of weird that we had two scheduled off days, which doesn't happen now except after the All-Star break. We won our 100th game in 12 innings, as I played in center and left. Not that anyone really wants extra innings at that point of the season. We lost on the last day of the season although I singled off relief pitcher Joe Decker. It was nice that none of the Cubs drilled us out of frustration, especially with a guy like Bill Hands starting the last game. Gil started the regulars again. Cleon finished with a .340 average, third behind Pete Rose and Roberto Clemente.

Towards the end of the season, we were on the plane and Gil asked the team who had played in the most games. Who was in the top five? People were surprised that I was one of them. He'd come up with little things out of the blue to keep us on our toes. He was a smart guy.

That 1969 pennant race is still one people talk about. In 1986, there was a "Dream Game" in Arizona for charity. They had the 1969 Mets play the 1969 Cubs. And we kicked their butts again, winning 11-3. And Ron Santo didn't show up because he said the memories of 1969 still hurt that much. It was 17 years later, and he still didn't like thinking about the Miracle Mets. A lot of guys did show up. Tom Seaver and Nolan Ryan didn't because they were still active players. But we had a nice turnout with Shamsky, Swoboda, Agee, Kranepool and other guys. I had an RBI single. And Ernie Banks and Ferguson Jenkins were playing for Chicago.

Winning the World Series

We were in the first ever NLCS, against the Atlanta Braves. I played in each game, although I didn't get to the plate. I was strictly a defensive replacement. We went into Atlanta confident like we always were. Everyone thought it was going to be a pitchers' duel with guys like Tom Seaver, Jerry Koosman, Phil Niekro and Pat Jarvis, but instead the games were high scoring. Our pitchers got knocked out, their pitchers got knocked out. Seaver got hit, Koosman got hit, Gentry got hit. We had a late rally to win the first game 9-5, and then we held on to win the second game 11-6 to take both games in Atlanta.

Gentry started game three. He was a textbook competitor who would challenge anybody with his fastball. He tried to throw a high fastball past Hank Aaron and Aaron tomahawked that ball over the centerfield fence at Shea Stadium. Not many guys could throw a fastball by 'bad Henry' but Gary would try. That tomahawk swing was Aaron being Hammerin' Hank. He had this down swing; he didn't really have an uppercut swing. That's how I learned to hit, hitting the ball on the ground, even if I didn't have any power like Aaron did. When you swing like that, you're swinging down a little bit, but when you hit the ball in that trajectory, you're putting that reverse spin on it and it takes off like a golf ball. The example I use, is if you have a nail, a piece of wood, and a hammer, when you hammer the nail into the wood, you don't throw your wrist facing up, you turn it over. And he would use his bat like a hammer.

Gentry got pulled in the middle of an at-bat in the third inning, but Nolan Ryan came in and pitched the rest of the way. Ken Boswell and Wayne Garrett homered and we won 7-4. We scored 27 runs in three games. The pitching staff for Atlanta wasn't very strong after Niekro.

For some reason, the NLCS is overlooked between the pennant race against the Cubs and the World Series. It's tough to even find footage from the games.

So again we get to celebrate at Shea. And I'm talking to Lindsey Nelson. I mouthed off. "We're going to beat Baltimore four straight." I'm sure when Baltimore got a hold of that they went crazy. They must have been thinking, 'Who's that rookie mouthing off like that?' Frank Robinson said, "Who the hell is Ron Gaspar?" I didn't care about that. It didn't bother me. I am sure losing to the Mets has bothered Frank all these years. What a great baseball player he was. I know the word "competitive" is overused now days, but to me he was one the best and the most competitive player in our era. He could play on my team anytime.

Before the World Series began, Clendenon grabbed me and said, "Come here Rodney, I want you to meet someone." He pushed me in front of Frank Robinson. I looked at him and he looked at me. That was it. I don't remember if we even shook hands, probably not. I respect people. As far as I'm concerned, we're all the same. Nobody is more special than anyone else, at least not in GOD's eyes. We just have a few more life experiences.

Don Buford led off Game One with a home run against Tom Seaver and Baltimore tacked on some more runs later on. Most people thought they would beat us easily and then Buford homers right away. I thought Swoboda should've caught the ball and I think he'd tell you that too. He comes into the dugout and is complaining about not catching it and Kranepool says to him, "Why don't you shut the f--- up? Don't worry, you'll get them next time." That's Kranepool. There's no mincing words there, just "shut the f--- up." They had been good friends for years, so he could talk to him like that. Swoboda was OK and that was it.

We were down 4-0 heading into the seventh. We scored once and had a rally going. Gil sent me in as a pinch-hitter against Mike Cuellar with two on and two out. It was a bit cold and I wasn't real loose. I'm in the batters' box and Elrod Hendricks was a talker like a lot of catchers were. You just try to ignore him because they try to distract you and get your mind off the game. He said, "Hey, Rod. You nervous?" I said, "No. I'm doing fine." He goes, "How come your knees are shaking?" Yeah, right.

It's hard to pinch-hit when you haven't played in a few days and you're sitting on the bench and facing a pitcher like Cuellar. I tip my hat to guys like Manny Mota and Lenny Harris who were so good at pinch-hitting. (I wasn't one of those guys.) It takes a special talent. Cuellar threw me a sinker low and away, and I hit a little dribbler to third. Brooks Robinson grabs it, makes a good play and throws me out. I always said it was my own fault that I was thrown out because I wasn't warmed up. If I was warmed up, I feel I would have beaten throw to first. I was thrown out by at least two steps. And usually when you're swinging like that, you're leaning towards first base. So you should get a decent jump out of the box, but I didn't for some reason. To this day, I think I should have beat that ball out. You can always think, I should've done this, I should've done that, but I didn't, so no excuses. Then Brooks made the same play on Grote in the next game.

When they selected the All-Century Team in 1999, Brooks Robinson was one of the third basemen, along with Mike Schmidt. There was a film on the 30 players on the team, about two minutes for each player. One of the Robinson highlights they used was his play throwing me out.

I was on the cover of Sports Illustrated, with me at the plate and Robinson at third. My daughter, a few years ago for a birthday present, put the magazine in a plaque and did a nice job. For a guy who didn't play all the time, I got a lot of publicity for different things. For the cover, the camera was really focused on Brooks at third but I was the one hitting. I did get a lot of ink for whatever reason.

We won game two, with Ed Charles, Al Weis and Jerry Grote coming through with hits in the ninth to put us up 2-1. Koosman pitched great but walked two batters in the ninth, so Gil brought Ron Taylor in to pitch to Brooks Robinson. Ed made the last play, short-hopping a grounder and then going to third to tag the base but it was too late so he threw to Clendenon and it was a errant throw which Clendenon picked out of the dirt.

In a one-run game, Gil used a four-man outfield against Frank Robinson in the ninth inning, sending Al Weis to left field. You knew Frank wasn't going to bunt. It wasn't a bunting situation. The Orioles need a home run, not a bunt. He ended up walking. Gil also made the decision to take Koosman out, one out away from the win. Taylor was a sinkerball pitcher and Brooks hit it on the ground to third, so it made sense.

We returned home to play the next three games. I picked up my parents who were coming in from Hawaii, and I just parked my car right out in front of the airport. Some cop who knew me was there and he said, "Hey Rod, just leave your car here,

I'll watch it for you." So I just left it there, went in and got my parents and away we went. My dad cracked up and said, "You got a cop watching your car for you?" They thought that was the greatest thing.

All these celebrities were at the games at Shea, not that I met any of them. Jackie Kennedy Onassis, Jerry Lewis and Pearl Bailey were a few of the stars who came to watch us. Pearl sang the national anthem before Game Five. And there was Karl Ehrhardt, known as the "Sign Man" at Shea Stadium. This guy would hold up these huge signs for every occasion. He really added to that great atmosphere at the ballpark.

Gary Gentry and Jim Palmer were the starting pitchers in Game Three. Tommie Agee hit a leadoff homer and made two great catches that saved five runs. They were both clutch plays, no doubt about it. The first one, he took a two-run double away from Elrod Hendricks with a running back handed grab at the 396 sign. Before the pitch, on the NBC camera angle you can see Agee in right-center. He had to run a long way to left-center, which is why I think that one is the better play. And then a few innings later with the bases loaded, he made a diving catch in right-center to rob Paul Blair. I thought he misjudged the second one a little bit, maybe because of the wind. He had to dive for it. To me, with it being to his glove hand, I thought that would be an easier play. But he made the diving catch. That's the 1969 Mets. We always made the play when we had to make it.

I pinch-hit in the eighth inning and flew out to left against Dave Leonhard. Then I stayed in the game in right field and caught the first two outs of the ninth inning. We won that game 5-0 to go up 2-1 in the series.

The next day, Seaver led 1-0 going into the ninth and two singles put runners on the corners with Brooks Robinson up. He lined one to right and Swoboda made the greatest catch I've ever seen for an outfielder. Ron is the only one who would try to dive for a ball like that. He made himself a good outfielder. Years later, he told me that it ticked him off to no end that I would go in for him as a defensive replacement in games earlier in the season. Ron told me that he worked his tail off and before games he had our third-base coach, Eddie Yost, hit him 100 fungos at a time because he was working on his defense. I didn't replace him as much later in the year, and not in Game Four of the World Series. He became a good outfielder but it just fried his butt that Gaspar was replacing him for defensive purposes late in games. I don't blame him. That's what being a competitor and being a ballplayer is all about. Heck, nobody wants to be taken out, but he worked hard and it paid off big-time. If you watch the full play, he not only caught it but rolled over, came up and threw a rocket to home plate. He didn't get the runner as Frank Robinson tagged up and scored to tie the game. It was a good all-around play. Had the ball Brooks hit got past Swoboda, it's a whole new ballgame. It probably would've been a triple and Baltimore would've led 2-1.

In the bottom of the 10th, Grote reached on a pop-fly double that I thought Don Buford should have had. Buford went back on it at first but it landed right in front of him. Shea Stadium was tough and it was hard to pick the ball up. Jerry was hustling all the way. Grote had good speed for a catcher. He ran very well but I guess I was a little faster, so I pinch-ran for Jerry. I was ready to pinch-run and was anticipating to do so if Jerry got on.

Earl Weaver had Dick Hall intentionally walk Al Weis to put runners on first and second with Seaver due up. Gil used J.C.

Martin to pinch-hit for Seaver, and Weaver brought in Pete Richert, a lefty.

It was an obvious bunt situation. Seaver was a good bunter in his own right, but Gil put Martin in. Every move Gil made worked that year. It was a sacrifice to get me to third. If the bunt is popped up, I have to freeze so that I don't get doubled off. Or there is always the chance the bunt is popped up but the fielder lets it drop, like Seaver actually did on a play earlier in the game. Even if it's an in-between play, you can't really go until you know it's going to drop in for sure.

J.C. laid down a perfect bunt that Richert picked up and threw to first, but it hit J.C. in the wrist and rolled towards second base.

I'm going to third on this. Keep in mind that you can't hear anything. There are 55,000 people there. I'm at third and Eddie Yost is two feet from me, yelling at me to run and I can't hear him. It wasn't until I turned around, looked over my shoulder, and saw the ball rolling towards second base that I took off. Eddie was right to yell at me to go. I just hesitated because I couldn't hear him. Our daughter, Taylor, got me a framed picture of me scoring the run. I was running well on that play, compared to how I ran in the first game. I could have walked home because there were no Orioles even near the ball. Seaver was the first one out of the dugout to congratulate me. Seaver was very aware of everything that was going on. That was his one World Series win. He congratulated me, and then the other guys came over.

Martin had put down a super bunt and maybe Richert was thrown off because he and the catcher both went to pick it up. People remember that one because it was a controversial play. Some people thought it was interference because Martin was in the baseline, but they didn't overturn it, which they shouldn't have. Replay is a pet peeve of mine. I hate seeing officials overturn plays or going to review a replay. I'm not a fan of that. Sometimes there's going to be human error in your favor; sometimes it's going to be in the other teams' favor. Thankfully they didn't overturn it in our case. Now with replay, you never know, maybe they would've changed the call.

Now we're up 3-1 in the series and have a chance to clinch at home with Jerry Koosman on the mound. In the third inning, the opposing pitcher, Dave McNally, hit a home run. And then Frank Robinson, who was having a terrible series (none of those guys hit well for Baltimore), hit one and Baltimore led 3-0. Koosman came back to the dugout and said, "Boys, go get them because they're not getting another run off me. I'm going to hold them the rest of the way," which he did. We wanted to win game five at home and not go back on the road. I think we knew we were going to win that day. But we didn't want to go back to their home field because momentum can change very quickly.

In the fifth, Frank Robinson got hit by a pitch and they wouldn't give him first base. The umpire said it hit his bat first. So Robinson held up the game to get checked in the clubhouse and then Koosman struck him out.

In our half of the sixth, the Shoe Polish play happened. I was right there about six or seven feet from Gil. Koosman, sitting next to Gil, later said Gil asked him to rub the ball on his shoe. I was sitting right on the dugout steps by the corner and Gil is sitting at the end of the bench and there's a ball bag there. When it happened, I had a good view of it. I was a pretty good cheerleader from my spot on the dugout steps.

Cleon looks like he gets hit and he starts walking to first. Home plate umpire Lou DiMuro said that the pitch didn't hit Jones. Cleon said it hit his foot, and Clendenon came from the on-deck circle to say it hit Cleon. The umpire still didn't change the call.

The ball rolls into the dugout and I turn around and see Gil reach in the bag and pull out a ball with shoe polish on it. You put your hand in a bag, nobody can see which ball you're grabbing. It might have been the ball that hit Cleon's foot, but I don't know if it was. Gil just pulled a ball out of there. Gil showed the ball to DiMuro and he gave Cleon the base. It probably was the game ball, but who knows? I was as close to Gil as anyone when it happened. That's my story and I'm sticking to it.

Then Clendenon hits a bomb. Al Weis, who had never hit a home run at Shea, hits one to tie it in the seventh. Isn't that something? Clutch player...The Amazing Mets! He only hit six home runs in his career up to that point, but one of them had been off McNally. There's a picture of me, Seaver and Clendenon congratulating him as he comes back to the dugout.

That's the kind of team we had. I mean, Al Weis? He hit two home runs the entire year but then he hits one in the World Series. Clutch hitter, great defensive ballplayer, hit .455 in the World Series. That's the kind of team we had, and I think that's one reason people remember us so much, because we would do things that teams had never done before, especially as a 100-1 underdog.

We took the lead in the bottom of the eighth. Cleon led off with a double off the wall in left-center, which almost went out. If you watch Cleon's swing, it looks like he just threw his hands out and actually hit it one handed. But he got his hands out and the ball hit the good part of the bat. Of course Cleon was very strong. I couldn't do something like that. But guys now think you have to swing from your butt, and you don't. You don't have to swing hard to hit the ball well.

Clendenon came up and was asked to bunt. We were all good bunters. It's funny that Gil didn't care that Donn had hit three home runs in the series, and one of those had been in his prior at-bat. But Donn couldn't get it down, and then swung away and grounded out to third.

Then Swoboda hit one down the line in left that Buford couldn't get. Everyone remembers Ron's diving catch, but few remember that he hit .400 in the series. Then we added an insurance run on a Baltimore error.

Davey Johnson came up with two outs in the ninth as the tying run and he drove one to left field. I was concerned when he hit it. But then Cleon Jones stopped going back and caught it. I thought Johnson hit it pretty well. I was sitting next to Yogi, and while the ball was in the air Yogi said, "That's the game." Later on, I asked Yogi how he knew. He said that he could just tell when Davey hit it that it wasn't going out. Yogi would know.

For the third time in a month, we ran on the field with all the fans at Shea. The fans flooded the field. I've never seen so many people on a field. I was going out to celebrate with my teammates and a few of the fans ran into me, and I got knocked down. I looked up and see all of these crazy people. I saw this guy in a dark uniform, who I thought was a cop, and he helped me up and got me to the clubhouse. Years later, I was looking at pictures and saw that it was actually umpire Lee Weyer who helped me. He was getting people out of the way so that I could run into the dugout. Weyer was a big guy, about 6' 6". I always wanted to thank him but never did get the chance, because by the time I saw the picture of Lee helping me, he had already passed.

The only thing that compares to that crowd was later that year on New Year's Eve and this girl I was with wanted to go to Times Square. It was so crowded near midnight and the crowd started moving, and she started sinking. They're pressing up on her and I got her up and was trying to knock people away so we could get out of there. It's scary when a mob is around you. There's not much you can do.

It was the best place to play. People loved us, and we loved them. The fans in the city never forget. The New York people know more about my time there than I did.

In the clubhouse, Lindsey Nelson said, "Well, Rod, you won four straight." I said, "We did, Lindsey. I didn't say which four." They didn't have a chance to beat us, just like everybody else who played us. Other than Seaver and Koosman and a few others, there were a lot of no-names, but when you put us on the field we played well together. Baltimore had no chance against us. Nobody did against our team that year. Especially for the last two months.

It was like the Cubs again. If you put our teams on paper, you'd think they would crush us. No way. You don't win games on paper. You go out there and play. We were so young, we didn't care who the heck these guys were and the names they had. Atlanta had Rico Carty, Orlando Cepeda and Hank Aaron. But you don't win games individually, you win collectively, with a good, solid team that knows how to play the game. And Gil Hodges taught us how to play the game.

When I compete in any sport, I always like to go against the big name, the famous guy, and I love beating up on them.

After we had won the series, Seaver went into Gil's office and poured some champagne on his head. Not too much, just a little. They had smiles on their faces. They were two Marines who had a lot of respect for each other.

For the World Series shares, guys got $18,338.18. Other players who weren't on the postseason roster got money. Amos Otis received a half-share. A bunch of guys who came up late in the season got some money. A number of Mets were voted $100 shares. Jim Bibby was called up late in the season and received a share, even though he didn't pitch in any games. A few years later, Whitey Herzog was managing the Rangers and traded for Bibby because he liked him from his Mets days. Bibby helped the Pittsburgh Pirates win the World Series in 1979.

Les Rohr, who was a high draft pick, got $100. Bob Johnson, who was an excellent pitcher with Pittsburgh and helped the Pirates win the 1971 World Series, received $100. Mike Jorgensen didn't play in any games in 1969 but had been called up and received some money. Bob Heise received $100. Jim Gosger was an outfielder who didn't play in the postseason, and then he returned to the Mets in 1973, but again wasn't on the postseason roster. What are the odds of that?

Somebody involved with the World Series paperwork for our check asked me where I wanted to put my hometown. I told them New York. I got a check for something less than $10,000. That's how much tax they took out. And I'm going, 'Wait a minute.' So I asked if I could put down a different city and they said I could. So I put down Kailua, Hawaii, where my parents lived. I got another $2,000 back, which was nice. Later on, I was doing my income tax and there was a category for Income Averaging at the time, and I ended up getting some more money back. For a guy who never had much money, I learn real quick how to do the proper paperwork for tax reasons.

Photo 1 of 2: Scoring the winning run in the bottom of the tenth inning, giving the Mets and Tom Seaver the win, 2-1.

Photo 2 of 2: Scoring the winning run in the bottom of the tenth inning in Game Four, giving the Mets and Tom Seaver the win, 2-1. Mets are up three games to one.

Greeted at home plate by Tom Seaver and Jerry Grote.

With Bobby Valentine as Hawaii Islander teammates in 1976.

With Mickey Mantle at an insurance convention in Southern California, comparing World Series rings.

At Citi Field for the 1969 Mets 40th reunion in 2009.

With Bob Pfeil in Barcelona, Spain 'fighting' a bull on a trip with some of the Mets to Europe, January, 1970.

With Ken Boswell singing with Don Ho in Honolulu, Hawaii, November 1969.

In Zurich, Switzerland, after 'winning' the Dating Game, January, 1970.

With Lindsey Nelson and Bob Murphy and their wives in Rabat, Morocco, January, 1970.

With coach Eddie & Pat Yost, Bob & Melanie Pfeil, Jerry & Sharon Grote, Wayne Garrett and Sargent Shriver on Europe trip.

With my bride Sheridan, and Tom and Nancy Seaver and Ruth and Nolan Ryan at 40th reunion.

Sheridan and I on our wedding day, July 7, 1970.

Sheridan and I at home in Mission Viejo, Ca. I love that flag.

Life as a Champion

After we won the World Series, "The Dating Game" contacted the Mets and wanted to know if we had three single guys to appear on the program. So Kenny Boswell, Wayne Garrett and I were on "The Dating Game." Everybody else on the '69 Mets was married so that's how we got picked. None of us were very excited about being on the program but we went out to Los Angeles to film it. I won on "The Dating Game", if you could call it winning. The gal picked me to go to Switzerland, which I did. I had nothing else to do at that time, so I went to Zurich. It was supposed to be a skiing trip. We were there five days and I think we were on the slopes maybe one hour. I'm not a skier, still not.

After it was done, Kenny and I went to Hawaii because that's where my parents lived at the time. We went to the Don Ho Show and they called me and Boswell up on stage to sing.

We also had a cruise in the Mediterranean Sea. We were in Morocco and Spain. It was Wayne Garrett, Bobby Pfeil and his wife, Jerry Grote and his wife, Eddie Yost and his wife, Lindsey Nelson and his wife. At one point they had us fighting these baby bulls in Spain. They asked if we wanted to hold the cape and deal with these bulls. It wasn't like I was a matador dealing with a real dangerous thing. I'm holding a bottle of wine with one hand, so I probably wasn't in much of a condition to be fighting a bull. So I'm running away from a little, stupid baby bull.

We were all over the place. Mayor Lindsay had us at Gracie Mansion and we saw Governor Rockefeller at his mansion. We met all the big wheels. It was probably because of us that Lindsay got reelected. He wasn't going to win but we got him that second term. There are pictures of me pouring champagne on his head in the locker room. He asked me and Ron Swoboda to speak at one of his rallies, which we did. Lindsay was a nice guy and I liked him. He seemed to be a normal guy and not standoffish. He had lost in the primary election but then ran on another line and won a few weeks after we won the World Series. He took advantage of it and why not? He made a joke denying that we had anything to do with his victory, and any further questions should be addressed to Deputy Mayor Hodges.

We were on the "Ed Sullivan Show." As a team we went on stage and sang "You Gotta Have Heart." As baseball players, you're performers. You are playing seriously but you're performing like an actor does. I took a public speaking class in high school. I hated it. After playing baseball, it's amazing how many guys who were quiet and reserved end up being speakers because they were exposed to crowds as athletes. It's another good learning experience as far as having confidence to speak to groups of people or people in general.

There weren't any takes of "You Gotta Have Heart." How long does it take to sing? Three minutes? I still have the "You Gotta Have Heart" album, although I don't know if it works anymore. There are no record players around.

A few of the Mets had a little show in Vegas where they sang: Agee, McGraw, Swoboda, Clendenon, Kranepool and Shamsky. Years later, a few of them were on "Everybody Loves Raymond." In the show, Raymond's dog was named Shamsky and the producers actually got Art and a few of the guys on the program. That's how New York works. There's no other place like it.

At 23 years old, I experienced so much as a rookie in New York. Who wins a World Series as a rookie playing in New York City?

It was a great time in our country and we need more great times like that in this country. A lot happened in 1969: Woodstock, man landing on the moon, the Mets winning the World Series. Economically speaking, New York was in terrible shape. People were down, but the Mets seemed to lift everybody's spirits. The Jets had won the Super Bowl in January and the Knicks won the NBA title the following May and we beat the Orioles in the World Series.

It was like a dream, like it never happened. Then you look back and realize it did happen. We have film and books to prove that we did win in 1969. And I was on that team. People would say to me, "Rod, you're famous." I don't think I'm famous. I was on a famous team though. People remember the 1969 Mets and they always will.

The fans never forget. I'm good with signing autographs. People find my address and they send me memorabilia. I'll sign a couple of things but some people like to take advantage.

I learned more that year than any other. I think traveling and seeing different places and people is the best education you can get. And we traveled all over, and would have been more if they had interleague play like they do now. When you're around different areas of the country and different types of people, that's how you learn. I still tell young people to go to school and get their education if they can, as opposed to rushing to play in a professional league that will still be there when they finish school, even if the educational system isn't perfect in this country. A lot of these schools teach these kids to be activists instead of giving them an education. These kids go out and protest and I don't even think they know what they're protesting. The parents are putting them through school to be a protestor? So many people want a free hand. Free this, free that. But if you have an opportunity to travel, do it. Even if you have to take a year off from school, and then go back. I got to do all that traveling for free. That was my best education. I never traveled at all until I signed a pro contract, and I got to experience a lot of nice things throughout the country.

Who can imagine a kid out of Lakewood High School in California, meeting the governor and mayor of New York, and attending luncheons at their places? That just doesn't happen. Well, I could play baseball a little bit, so that's why it happened. It's just another reason why baseball is so great.

No Encore

I figured I'd be good to play in 1970. Gil wanted me to play winter ball in Venezuela but I wasn't going there. I was still thinking about my experience in Mexico. Baseball-wise, it's one of the worst decisions I ever made. I had a nickel-brain. I played year round since I was seven years old up until that point. After winning the World Series I figured I'd stay in New York and make some money. What a bunch of hogwash that was. So I didn't go down to play winter ball. I didn't do anything all winter long as far as working out, throwing, hitting, etc.

I went to spring training in 1970 and I was awful. I deserved to be sent down. I couldn't hit. I couldn't catch fly balls. It was immaturity on my part. I didn't realize that once you get to the big leagues, it's a lot easier getting there than staying there. Especially when you're coming off your rookie season like I was and you're with an organization like the Mets, which had some tremendous ballplayers in their farm system. They were developing guys like Tim Foli, Leroy Stanton (who was sent to the Angels in the Nolan Ryan trade), Ken Singleton, and Jon Matlack. And I just took it for granted that I would be in the big leagues for at least the next 10 years because I had been on a World Championship team.

That's not how it works. You've got to bust your butt and perform or they're going to get rid of you. I don't recommend guys slacking off like I did and I paid the price in baseball. So they sent me down, and the next day I met my future wife, Sheridan. Although I didn't know it at the time, it was a big-time blessing that the Mets sent me to the minor leagues. If I had made the big club, I probably would have never met my bride. Although I wasn't a Christian at the time, GOD had a great plan for me with Sheridan. Over the years we have been blessed tremendously in all areas of our life. We are in our 49th year of marriage and our life, LORD willing, continues to be a big-time blessing. In my opinion she is the reason for our successful marriage and us having five great kids and ten wonderful grandchildren.

I did get back to the big leagues but not for an extended period of time. It's my own fault. I worked very hard to get there in 1969. I worked hard in elementary school, junior high, high school, college and my first years in pro ball. Well, I'm at the top. I don't have to work that hard anymore. I was complacent at the wrong time in my life. I didn't get 10 years in the big leagues but I got parts of four, which is more than most people have.

I was one of the last guys to sign in 1970. Who am I? Come on, I'm like the 20th guy on the roster, maybe lower, and I'm one of the last to sign. I went from $10,000 in 1969 to $19,000 in 1970, which was my top salary for all the years I played.

Like I said, in spring training I was awful. I hadn't picked up a baseball in four months. I had been playing year-round since I was seven years old. But I didn't have the maturity to realize that it's easier to get to the big leagues than to stay in the big leagues. I still figured I would make the club. Obviously I was wrong.

Jack Lang was one of the big sportswriters in that era. He was the man who would call players when they were elected into the Hall of Fame because he was the Executive Secretary for the Baseball Writers' Association of America. During spring training he wrote that Gaspar was playing baseball like he's still on "The Dating Game." I got ticked off when I read that, but he was right. I was terrible. I was sent down to the minors. I didn't deserve to make it.

I had made it to the majors pretty quickly, maybe too quickly. Whitey Herzog thought that they should have kept me down another year, but I'm not complaining.

The funny thing is that the guy who replaced me was Dave Marshall, who they had acquired in the offseason. I grew up with him in Lakewood even though he was a few years older than I was. He was a heck of an athlete. I think he was the best athlete to come out of Lakewood High School. He lettered in baseball, football, basketball and track. One time during a baseball game, in between innings he got permission from the coach to go over to the track meet and participated in the long jump and he won it. He won the long jump in between innings. Then he went back to playing in the baseball game. He was a tremendous athlete.

He had a good spring, I had a miserable spring, and that was it. I still remember Gil calling me in to tell me I wasn't going to be with the team. It got to me. It broke me down a little bit. I wasn't the happiest guy in the world but it worked out well.

Tidewater was nice. The team had a new ballpark. I started losing a little interest in the game after I got married, which is my fault. Sometimes guys say, "I had a bad break here, I had a bad break there." Guys make their own breaks. I deserved being in AAA Tidewater. I didn't have the same fire I had in 1969. After the World Series, I got a little lax.

Chuck Hiller was the manager. When he was with the Giants, Hiller was the first National League player to hit a grand slam in World Series history. He was alright. We had our clashes. He wasn't made to manage. He had run-ins with a few guys. Chuck was a hard-nosed guy.

In 1969, I had made the club on my birthday, April 3. In 1970, I was sent down on my birthday.

If I had gone to Venezuela like Gil wanted me to, I would've been in shape and probably have made the team out of spring training. But then I wouldn't have met my wife.

I met Sheridan through a friend of mine who I played baseball with, Ronnie Paul. Ronnie and his family had an apartment close to the facility in spring training. He told me there were a couple of single girls living across the street from him. So I went over there with Danny Frisella, the Met pitcher. Sheridan had been skeptical of ballplayers because she heard that a lot of them were married. I wasn't married and we started hanging out together.

There's a funny thing about Sheridan's parents seeing me play. This was while Sheridan and I were dating. There was a game in Toledo against the Mud Hens, and her parents were from Ohio. They drove down to watch me. So they're at the game and I'm in the lineup, and I'm leading the league in hitting. On that day, with her parents there, I get thrown out of the game. I hadn't even met them yet. I don't know what kind of impression that made on them. That was the only time they ever saw me play.

I was usually fine with the umpires. Remember that the umpires in the minor leagues are trying to make it to the majors just like the players are. Fred Brocklander was very inconsistent behind the plate but he made it to the major leagues. So somebody liked him. But he struggled a little bit in the field. Mets fans might remember him calling an Astros runner out at first when the Houston runner was safe in a 1986 playoff game. That cost the Astros a run.

Terry Cooney was an umpire who threw me out of a game in Phoenix one time. He said, "Say another word and I'm throwing you out." And I said something and he threw me out. He thought it was a strike, I didn't think it was a strike, back and forth, wham, I'm gone. He wasn't going to take it. Cooney ejected Roger Clemens from a 1990 playoff game, with the Red Sox facing elimination no less. He didn't like the players talking back to him. None of the umpires did.

The best balls-and-strikes umpire was Dutch Rennert. He was very consistent. You never argued with him because he was usually right. Dutch was very loud. You knew when it was a strike for sure. He had something going against him, which I think delayed his time getting to the big leagues, which was that he wasn't very tall. The league always wanted big guys to be umpires in the majors. But Dutch was such a good umpire that they had to get him up there, and they called him up eventually. He was only around 5' 8" but he was one of the best. Paul Runge was a good one who had come from an umpiring family. His dad, Ed, had been an ump.

The Tidewater team had Ron Allen, Dick's brother. There was Larry Bearnarth, who had pitched for the Mets in the early '60s and later became a pitching coach with the Expos and Rockies. Randy Bobb was a catcher we had acquired from the Cubs before the season.

Another catcher was Steve Chilcott. He was a buddy of mine in spring training, a nice kid. He had been the number one overall pick in 1966, one spot ahead of Reggie Jackson, but he never made it to the big leagues. Steve was a big, strong catcher who could throw but he couldn't really hit. He hurt his shoulder diving into a base, but he had a good arm before that. He was the nicest guy. I'm not even sure if he got into any games at the Triple-A level. Of course, if the Mets had picked Reggie over Chilcott, I might not have been on the 1969 Mets.

Bill Denehy started a number of games for us. He was the Met pitcher sent to Washington for Gil Hodges after the 1967 season. We had Rich Folkers, who was a number one pick with the Mets in 1967. He was a good, left-handed pitcher who was in the big leagues for a while. Jesse Hudson was a reliever who pitched in one game with the 1969 Mets, and never made it back to the majors. He was a tall, slim lefty who could throw hard.

There was reliever Danny Frisella, who was my roommate. Sheridan and I saw his wife a couple of years ago. Danny died in a tragic dune buggy accident New Year's Day, 1977.

Ed Kranepool was sent down to Tidewater. He was hitting under .120 in late June. Ed regained his hitting stroke and was called up shortly thereafter.

I was having an All-Star season and on July 6, the International League All-Stars had an exhibition game in Norfolk against the Baltimore Orioles. Some of those Orioles made some comments towards me, not that I cared much. They must've gotten some satisfaction that the guy who said the Mets would win four in a row against them in the World Series was down in the minor leagues. I led off against Dave Leonhard, who had given up a home run to Ed Kranepool in the World Series. I doubled off the wall in right-center off Leonhard. We won the game in the ninth on a single from Angel Manuel. Angel was later on the A's teams that won three World Series titles in a row, and he had the game-winning hit against the Reds in one of those games. His brother, Pepe, played a bit for the Mets. With that win, I had beat the Orioles again.

After the All-Star Game, Sheridan and I were married the next day. I had met her in April, and the actual time we spent together had been 10 days. I knew if I ever married I would not have a long engagement. I wouldn't give the girl a chance to get out of it. After the season, Sheridan and I lived in Hawaii with my parents. My parents loved Sheridan.

Nice numbers to remember: 7/7/70. Ronnie Paul was the best man. We had a doubleheader scheduled the day I was married. I said, "I'm not going to the ballpark. I just got married." So I didn't go. I told the general manager, Dave Rosenfield. And Rosenfield told Chuck Hiller. And Hiller went crazy. We battled occasionally. He wanted to fine me and do whatever he could to me. He was mad as heck. Dave talked Chuck out of fining me and told him that I had just gotten married and to let me have a day off. I don't even know if Hiller knew I was getting married. Dave was a good guy, who passed away recently. I was still a Met prospect and at that point in July, I was leading the International League in hitting. So I was having a pretty good year. It was tough for Chuck to do much to me.

I finished the season in Tidewater hitting .318, which was near the top of the league. Future Brave Ralph Garr led the league in hitting. Sheridan always blamed herself for Garr winning the batting title. She says, "Well, if you hadn't married me, then you would have hit a lot higher." I don't think so. I had just lost a little interest in baseball at that time. I was disappointed in myself. I never blamed the Mets, or anybody else for anything that happened. I don't believe in excuses unlike a lot of people in general, where it's always somebody else's fault. Statistically, it was probably my best year in professional baseball. I won a Silver Glove, which is the minor league equivalent of the Golden Glove. I made one error, on a ball hit in front of me, which I tried to make a shoestring catch on and it hit the tip of my glove and fell out, and they gave me an error on it.

I was called up to the Mets in September. I led off a few times against the Phillies, including once against Jim Bunning. There were a few new faces with the Mets. Tim Foli was the number one overall pick in 1968 who was sent right to Double-A Memphis when I was there. He was a very good ballplayer, who had been called up from Tidewater. Leroy Stanton and Ken Singleton were both called up from Tidewater and made their debuts. (Funny thing about that group is that they were all traded within a few seasons. Singleton and Foli to the Expos for Rusty Staub, and Stanton to the Angels in the Nolan Ryan deal for Jim Fregosi.)

In 1969, I was behind Agee, Jones and Swoboda with Shamsky also on the bench. In September 1970, it was those guys plus Stanton and Singleton and Marshall. It's like competing for time in an eight-man outfield. There was a game where Stanton led off with a triple but the relay throw drilled him in the head and I went in as a pinch-runner. Leroy was a good guy who was sent to the Angels along with Nolan Ryan and had himself a decent career. What a trade that was. Leroy was a good, strong outfielder who could run. He had some pop and had the nicest smile on his face all the time. He led the expansion Seattle Mariners in home runs in their first season.

Another new Met in 1970 was Joe Foy. The team traded Amos Otis to the Royals to get him. What a travesty that was. Joe had some drug issues. Amos was a top prospect and the team wanted him to play third, which he didn't want to do. He ended up becoming an All-Star outfielder and played better out there than anybody the Mets had. Amos was an All-Star four straight seasons from 1970-73. Foy came over after Ed Charles retired with the team still trying to solve the third-base problem they always had. Wayne Garrett played there for a lot of years and always did a good job. Wayne was easily a better ballplayer than Foy, although I guess they wanted a right-hander to platoon. Joe had his issues. I remember one time looking at his eyes and you can tell he was out there somewhere. Sadly, Foy died in the late '80s.

The Mets always had an issue finding a third baseman. They more than 40 guys there in the first eight years of the franchise. That hot-corner problem led to them trading Ryan to the Angels for Jim Fregosi, who had been an All-Star shortstop but had never even played at third before.

Mike Jorgensen was a good ballplayer from Queens. Mike was a local boy. He was a very good first baseman who could play the outfield, and was a good left-handed hitter. Mike had a 17-year career, and is the only position player who played for the Mets in the '60s, '70s, and '80s. We had Teddy Martinez, a young infielder from the Dominican Republic.

Shortly after being called up, I was in the lineup and faced Bob Gibson. Gibson would fall off the mound to the first base side with each pitch. So I'm thinking I'm going to bunt that ball right through the pitcher's mound. He threw a pitch right over the plate and he didn't even move. He knew what I was going to do ahead of time. I know he did. Instead of falling off, he was waiting for me. He could tell, and I don't know how because you don't telegraph a bunt single. I thought I'd be real clever and smart, and fool Gibson. Yeah, right. He fooled me. He was a great athlete.

118

On September 14, Gil used me as a pinch-runner in the 10th inning of a tie game in Montreal. I was observant as a base runner. I remember the first baseman taking off because he was expecting a bunt. So when he took off, I took off for second. I heard Gil yell, "Go!" around the same time I took off, so Hodges and I were thinking the same thing. I scored the go-ahead run and we went on to win 9-5.

We were tied for first place after that win, with 15 games to play. But there was no miracle in 1970. We lost 10 of our last 15 games and finished in third place. It just wasn't the same.

In 1969, wherever I went, everything was free. There was one diner I'd go to and I'd order corned beef hash and poached eggs, and the guy wouldn't take my money. The owner would just smile at me. The guy never talked, he just gave me my corned beef hash and eggs, and smile. I would also get free gasoline coupons. There was some place that gave us cars to drive. When you're winning, people give you free stuff.

I mean, it was incredible. There was one place in Midtown where I had clams casino for the first time, and I met the owner, who was a nice guy who I was told was mixed up with the mob. I don't know, but he treated me well. After we won the World Series, I went there with my parents and the restaurant took care of everything. And the owner and some of the workers would sing to us. It was great. Everywhere we went was fun.

In 1970, you go to all the same places, do all the same stuff and it's, "OK, here's your check."

You learn a lot. When you win, the world loves you. When you're not winning, it's a whole new ballgame. The world's a frontrunner and I understand that. I think we're all frontrunners at some time in our lives. Nothing could have topped 1969. Rod Gaspar is in the big leagues in his first year and winning the World Series, when a great guy like Ernie Banks didn't get to make it to the Fall Classic all those years he played. It doesn't seem fair.

It's hard to come back from a miracle year. Maybe the team was complacent and didn't have the drive it had the year before. It's hard to say. Maybe we had a cocky attitude. There was more pressure as well. We had none against the Cubs the year before, none against the Braves, none against the Orioles. We weren't expected to win anything. We were pretty loose. The expectations were higher in 1970. The Pirates and Cubs were tough. The National League had better ballplayers than the American League, as evidenced by the NL winning the All-Star Game every year.

I was traded to the Padres after the 1970 season. I could see the writing on the wall. I kind of liked it because I was going back to California, but again I didn't work out in the offseason that much and I wasn't in real good shape.

Surprisingly to me, the Mets wouldn't win another World Series with the same group of players who won in 1969. Gil died on April 2, 1972. That was two days before his 48th birthday. My birthday happened to be in the middle, on April 3. Gil was a young man. A number of those Brooklyn Dodgers died young. Jackie Robinson died in 1972 at 53. Junior Gilliam died in the late '70s. And Roy Campanella had his car accident, which ended his career.

We had a few guys die young, starting with our manager. Cal Koonce and Tommie Agee died in their 50s. Tommie tragically died of a heart attack in New York in 2001. He was only 58. As I get older, I think about those times and the fun we had, and wish I could be around them on a regular basis. But that's not how it works.

With all the young players, I thought the Mets could have gone a long way if Gil hadn't died. One day in Spring Training he went golfing with his coaches. After playing 18 holes, Gil said, "Let's play another 18," and he fell over backwards and was dead before he hit the ground. Joe Pignatano, his lifelong buddy, was right there with him. I think that was the downfall of the Mets, when we lost Hodges. With all the talent we had, we needed a good leader, and he was the best for us. With Gil out of the picture, things seemed to crumble over the next couple of years and culminated with them trading Seaver in 1977. Mets chairman M. Donald Grant wasn't the most popular man in New York after that.

People always say if Gil was around, they would've won more. It's amazing what one man can do, isn't it? Things went downhill in the front office and they made some bad trades, terrible trades. They sent Amos Otis to Kansas City, traded Nolan Ryan to the Angels and of all people, eventually trading Tom Seaver. M. Donald Grant was in charge by then, and he wasn't a baseball man like GM Bob Scheffing had been.

Whitey Herzog had left in the early '70s to go to the Texas Rangers. Some Mets fans think he should have been the manager in 1972. He was so knowledgeable and had been the third-base coach for a season before Hodges was the manager. And he ended up making the Hall of Fame as a manager. He won three pennants with the Cardinals, plus there were the three AL West titles he won with the Royals. Losing him hurt a lot, although Yogi Berra did manage the team to Game Seven of the 1973 World Series.

It's like any business. If you don't have good leaders, the business isn't going to do well. They had so much talent and the team was so young. We should've won a lot more pennants over the years.

San Diego and Hawaii

I learned quickly the Padres were not run like the Mets. During the winter, I got a call from Eddie Leishman, the San Diego Vice President. He offered me the same $19,000 I had made the year before and I wanted to negotiate. Leishman was a little nasty on the phone. He told me, "Alright, you don't want to sign a contract, stay in Hawaii." He didn't care and I had never met the guy before. That's how he treated you. You have to be kidding me. That was the first contact I had with the Padres, so I wasn't very impressed with them. They weren't the most pleasant people, probably because they were always finishing in last place since coming into the league in 1969.

Buzzie Bavasi was the president of the Padres. I wasn't a big fan of his, and I don't think he was a big fan of mine. I don't think most players were fans of his. He had a long career going back to his Brooklyn Dodgers days. He wasn't the most well-liked guy but he stayed in baseball a lot longer than I did so he must've done something better than I did.

Sheridan and I stayed in Hawaii that winter with my parents, who had a condo in Kailua, Hawaii. The Padres had me penciled in to play left field. I reported to this wonderful place, Yuma, Arizona, right in the middle of the desert. I remember Duke Snider was there because he was a broadcaster with the team. And I remember that he dyed his hair. I never really got to talk to him as one center fielder to another, or as guys who won in New York. But he was a good baseball announcer.

Again, I went to Spring Training out of shape and didn't make the club. They sent me down. You would think I would've learned my lesson from the year before.

Come on, the San Diego Padres? If I can't make that ballclub, then I can't make any club. They were only in their third year of existence. They weren't very good back then. As a matter of fact, they're not very good right now, either. The Padres weren't a good organization. And I'd come from the best one in baseball with the Mets. It was like night and day. Maybe they traded me over because they figured I was a California boy and I'd want to be on a California team, which is nice but it didn't make any difference to me.

I didn't deserve to make the team. Sounds like a replay from 1970. My attitude had changed again. I was irritated with baseball for not being in the majors for all of 1970. I was one of those crybaby baseball guys who thought baseball owed me a living, but it didn't. I realized that a year later when things came into focus and I thought that I should be happy to be playing this game. How could I ever complain about baseball? It had been good to me.

Once you blow two chances like I did in 1970 and 1971, it's hard to get any more.

They sent me down to the Triple-A club in Hawaii. We enjoyed it over there. Obviously, it's not bad to play in Hawaii. But it wasn't the big leagues. The ballpark was in downtown Honolulu, just this old rat-infested park. They had a big screen in right field that I always tried to hit the ball over but never did. There were some seats at ground level, so you'd be sitting and your head would be just above the ground watching the game. It was an interesting ballpark. Centerfield was well over 400 feet away from the plate. One game I was playing left field and I ran into the wall which was cement. I hurt my neck and had whiplash. So I go to the doctor who was this old Hawaiian guy, and his office wasn't the best-looking office in the world. I'm thinking, what am I doing here? I let him give me a shot in the neck, which somehow worked.

Bill Adair was the manager in Hawaii. He was a very easygoing, nice guy. As a player, he was a career minor leaguer but he had been on some major league coaching staffs, and had managed the White Sox for a week and a half in 1970. I only hit .275 that year, which wasn't a good year for me although it was one of the highest averages on the team. I had hit almost .320 the year before in Tidewater, in what was a pitchers' league. And then I bat .275 in a hitters' league. I don't know if I lost something or what, but I didn't have the kind of year I normally have. We had decent ballparks we played in, better than the International League. I did draw a lot of walks and finished with an on-base percentage over .400, the highest on the team.

Hawaii was like a stomping ground for former major leaguers. Over the years, the team would get guys who were over the hill so that they could draw fans. We had Clete Boyer, who had been the third baseman for the Yankees' pennant-winning teams of the early '60s. Clete was a former Gold Glove winner who could still field although he couldn't hit anymore.

Dennis Ribant, the former Met pitcher, led the Islanders in wins in 1971. He played six seasons in the majors, and pitched for six different teams. We called him The Weasel. He was a salesman type of guy. He finagled a Datsun 240-Z out of general manager Jack Quinn after the season because of his good year.

Bob Garibaldi won 11 games and later became a college basketball ref in the Pac-10. Bob had played at Santa Clara and was the Most Outstanding Player of the College World Series in 1962, and then later in the year he pitched on the Giants team that won the pennant although he didn't pitch in the World Series against the Yankees.

Steve Whitaker, the former Yankee outfielder, played for us. He would get so ticked off on the field. He was something. Miracle Met Jack DiLauro pitched for Hawaii.

Jim Hicks was our cleanup hitter. He was a big guy, a good hitting first baseman. Rich Barry was another good hitter, a big outfielder. We had Lee Maye, but not the one who played with the Reds. This one had played with the Braves in the '60s. Our third baseman was Rick Joseph, from the Dominican Republic.

One of my teammates was Tug McGraw's brother, Hank. Hank had been in the minors for about a decade. He was one of the first Mets bonus babies. Hank was in the system and he told them to sign his younger brother, and that's how the Mets signed Tug. Hank bounced around a lot and didn't always get along with management. He was a good guy who was one of the early hippies with the long hair and guitar. The Phillies had suspended him in 1970 because he didn't want to get his hair cut. He and Tug were a lot alike.

Leon Wagner was a former All-Star with the Angels, who was 37 years old when I was his teammate, a lefty hitter who could still swing the bat. He had originally signed with the Giants in the '50s and played for the Pacific Coast League's Hollywood Stars before the Dodgers moved out to California. He was a star with the Angels in the early '60s. People called him Daddy Wags. Hollywood stars and movie people would go to the games in Los Angeles. He was a very charismatic guy who was always smiling. He got to know the Rat Pack, Frank Sinatra, Dean Martin and Sammy Davis Jr. Leon told me about how they would go out and a different guy would pick up the tab each time. Leon told me when it came to his turn and he looked at the bill he thought he was in over his head. Money to those guys was nothing and they would do anything for a thrill, according to Wagner. They could pretty much do whatever they wanted.

Wagner later opened a haberdashery in Los Angeles. He was always a well-dressed guy. I found out later that he was living in the streets and he ended up dying in 2004. Had I known where he was I would have went to see him, but I didn't know. Guys get out of the game, and in a lot of cases, you don't know what happens to them.

I got called up at the end of the year, but so what? It wasn't the same. You get spoiled playing for the Mets. They had such a great organization and then I go to the Padres, which was like night and day. I have a little empathy for Buzzie because he was under financial restraints with the owner. That organization looked cheap compared to the Mets and Mrs. Payson. If you treat your players right, you're going to get good results. The Mets treated their players very well.

Preston Gomez was the manager. He was a good guy. There's one story about him which I think is classic. He was all baseball, very dedicated. I was told about a game the Padres played in Mexico during Spring Training and Preston had one of his friends throw batting practice before the game. The guy has a heart attack on the mound and dies. Preston sees this and goes 'OK, we need to keep going, get somebody else out there." His buddy just died of a heart attack and Preston was such a baseball guy that he wanted to continue batting practice. I cracked up when I heard that. It's kind of sad but that's Preston. Maybe this story is a little exaggerated but that is how it was told to me.

There were times Preston would announce a starting pitcher and have a different guy warming up in the bullpen, and then would bring him in during the first inning. He was always thinking of things. He was a good baseball man but he thought a little differently.

San Diego's jerseys weren't as classic as the Mets. Some of those colors they had were something else. I have a portrait of myself in a Padres uniform. I don't know who did it but it looks nice. At least it's not the yellow and brown colors they had later in the '70s, or the Diamondbacks jerseys now.

I couldn't wait for the season to be over. You wonder why they call you up when you hardly ever play. I played in 16 games and went 2-17, with three walks. And six of those at-bats came in one game. We lost the first game of a doubleheader in 21 innings. That's not what you want at that point of the season. The Padres were 2-14 in the 16 games I played as we were on our way to 100 losses.

Those aren't my fondest memories. There were times I preferred playing in Hawaii than San Diego because it was more fun. That was the wrong attitude. Why would you rather play in Hawaii, which is Triple-A ball, than San Diego, which is major league ball? But that was my attitude at the time. At least I was getting to play in warm cities.

After the pennant races of the previous two years with the Mets, it just wasn't exciting and much fun to play, especially when you're in last place. I remember sitting with Cito Gaston and Nate Colbert on the bench and they'd be talking, just hammering the Padres organization. It was classic. The Padres had some talent, but they couldn't win. Sometimes that happens.

Colbert was the top home run hitter on the team and was an All-Star. Ollie Brown was an outfielder with a Roberto Clemente-type arm, who had been the first-ever pick in Padres history. Mike Ivie was a catcher who had been a number one pick in 1970.

Enzo Hernandez and Don Mason were two little infielders. The organization loved Hernandez. I don't know why but they did for some reason. Infielder Garry Jestadt was a guy I hung out with, who became a real estate guy in the Phoenix area. Mike Caldwell and Fred Norman were good left-handed pitchers. Tom Phoebus, a 1969 Oriole, was on the team. He had won 14 games for Baltimore that year and was in consideration to start Game 4 of the World Series against the Mets although Mike Cuellar made his second start instead.

After 1971, it kicked in that I needed to get serious again. That winter I went back to California and got in shape in the offseason. In 1972, the players went on strike for the first time, pushing the start of the season back a week. Major League Baseball shut down. The Padres had frozen me and I was kind of in limbo about where I was going to play.

It was my worst year in baseball because I was in limbo and the Padres didn't know what to do with me. I began the year in Hawaii but then they shipped me to Indianapolis, the Triple-A affiliate of the Reds. They loaned my contract to them. There's a little difference between Indianapolis and Hawaii.

In Indianapolis, I played for Vern Rapp, who later became manager of the Cardinals, despite never playing or coaching in the majors. I didn't mind him although he was one of the hardest-nosed people I ever met in the game. He was fine as long as you played hard, and he didn't get on me for anything. His personality was a little abrasive for some guys though. Carroll Sembera, who struck me out on Opening Day 1969, was on that Indianapolis team, as well as a number of players who were with the Reds when they were winning pennants in the '70s.

It wasn't a good experience for me. I didn't like putting my family through all that. You don't like being away from them, especially in a place like Indianapolis, which was not the most pleasant place in the world. The American Association was the worst of the Triple-A leagues of that time. The Pacific Coast League was the best, then the International League, and then the American Association. The ballparks were not real good.

One day, I was watching the opposing outfielders throwing the ball lackadaisically to the shortstop, who took his time throwing it in. I'm on second base thinking how I'm going to tag up and score if there's a fly ball hit to the deep outfield with less than two outs. A ball was hit to deep centerfield, I tagged up and end up scoring from second base. Problem is, I tried to knock over the catcher, Dan Breeden, and he was waiting for me and knocked my shoulder out of place. But I did score. If I knew the shortstop's throw was going to short hop the catcher, I wouldn't have tried to knock the catcher over. I couldn't throw for a while after that and I missed a few games because I couldn't lift my left arm. That was really the only bad baseball injury I ever had. I guess it is good that I didn't play football. Kansas City Chiefs linebacker E.J. Houlb said that his knees looked like he lost a knife fight to a midget after all the surgeries he had. No thanks.

It was a terrible year for the Gaspar family. They were stuck back in California and I didn't have a good year at all. I hit .291

in Indianapolis and a disappointing .234 in Hawaii. I didn't play a lot and it reflected in my stats. I always hit well if I played regularly. I think if I played regularly in the major leagues I would've had a higher batting average. But I can't prove it because it didn't happen.

Rocky Bridges was the manager in Hawaii after Adair left following the 1971 season. Bridges had been an infielder in the majors for a decade and was an All-Star with the Senators. I was looking forward to playing for him but we never really got along. Everyone would tell stories about how Rocky Bridges was a really nice guy and how funny he was, which he was, but for some reason I don't think he cared for me too much. I have no idea why, because I had looked really forward to meeting him. I get along with people and Bridges had a good reputation. And he was a Long Beach guy too. That happens sometimes. If I had the answer for why we didn't get along better I would tell you, but I have no idea.

I usually hit .300 wherever I went but not that year. I hated it in Indianapolis, but it taught me a lesson. You've got to stay in shape if you're going to play this game. After 53 games with the Indians, I returned to Hawaii. It was a hectic time for Sheridan and I didn't really know what was going on in our baseball life.

One of my roommates in 1972 was Rick Stelmaszek. He was a great guy. He used to chew. When he would go to sleep, he would take it out, put it on the table next to the bed, and waking up the next morning he would put the sucker back in his mouth. It was also funny to ask him for the time. He had this accent being from the south side of Chicago. I'd ask him what time it was and he would say, "Something to 10." Or he'd go, "Something after 11." He wouldn't give the minutes because, if you think about it, that's close enough. The way he'd say it with his accent (which I can't imitate) and gravelly voice was so funny. He was a nice guy and was always smiling. Rick was a very good defensive catcher, and played in the big leagues for a bit. He later became the longest-tenured coach in Twins history. Sadly, he died of pancreatic cancer a few days after the 2017 World Series ended.

One of my Hawaii teammates, Al Severinsen, told me I should file a grievance because what the Padres did in sending me to Indianapolis was illegal. I don't know how he figured that one out but I go, "Oh, OK." So I filed a grievance against the Padres although I was still on their 40-man roster but not playing. At the time I was making $19,000 for the season which was better than the $10,000 I made for the 1969 Mets. The Mets almost doubled my salary in 1970, which I carried over to the Padres. So the Padres owed me money from the time I was in Indianapolis.

Bavasi caved in and ended up paying me the money that he owed me. That was nice. I don't know if it endeared me to the Padre front office but I was married and I needed the money. At the time, the Padres were always struggling financially. The owner was C. Arnholt Smith, who would eventually sell the team to McDonald's owner Ray Kroc. I was in Hawaii in 1973 and making about $2,000 per month to play Triple-A ball. And Hawaii was a pretty expensive place to live in 1973. And some poor kids who were in their first year of Triple-A were making $900 a month. Can you imagine that? And the rent was probably about half of that unless they were living with each other. I remember going on road trips in Hawaii and some of the younger guys like Billy Hodge, our catcher, would have their wives pack them peanut butter and jelly sandwiches to take on road trips because they didn't have any money to speak of. So that's what it was like playing in the Padres organization before Kroc took over.

After my disappointing season in 1972, I bounced back and hit .300 in 1973 with an on-base percentage over .400. It was a good year on and off the field.

That was also the year we bought our first home in Huntington Beach. I still remember that it cost $46,640. If I hadn't bought that when I did, Sheridan and I probably never would have owned a house because after that, the real estate prices started going up dramatically. At the time, it was a bit of a struggle because the house payments were a whopping $400 per month. At the time, that was a lot of money to us.

We had three different managers in 1973. Bridges was gone after 32 games. I don't remember if he left on his own or got fired. He later won a PCL title managing in the Giants system. Then we had Warren Hacker for a few games. Hacker pitched for the Cubs in the'50s. Then Roy Hartsfield was the manager in Hawaii. He had played a bit for the Boston Braves in the early '50s. He spent a lot of years as a player and then as a manager in the Dodgers' minor league system.

On the field, we had former Houston outfielder Brock Davis in left field as I played center. Davis had been one of the young guys in Houston in the early '60s when they had Rusty Staub, Jimmy Wynn, Joe Morgan and Jerry Grote. The catcher was Danny Breeden, who was the backstop who knocked my shoulder out the year before. Danny's brother, Hal, played with the Expos for a few years. We had Jack Hiatt, who spent almost a decade in the majors and was at the end of his career. Frank Johnson was a good right-handed hitter who had played with the Giants. Gene Martin was a left-handed hitter who had a cup of coffee with the Senators and later played in Japan.

My buddy Dave Marshall was on the team in Hawaii. That was his last year in pro ball and he was hurt all the time. At the end of the year he suffered two groin injuries, one on each side, and wasn't playing at all. He could hardly play at that point anyway, so on the last road trip of the year, Dave didn't even show up at the ballpark. He was nowhere to be found for those final games on the West Coast. He left and went to New York. That was it. He loved the environment in New York and I didn't see him for years. Years later he ended up in California and went into the security business.

In 1974, I made it back to the majors. First I started in Hawaii, with some good teammates. Right fielder Randy Elliott hit .321. John Scott was an outfielder who hit 12 home runs that year for the Islanders. Pat Corrales, the future manager, played for us. One time he got hit in the head, went down, got right back up and went down to first base without saying a word. He wasn't much of a hitter but he was a really good catcher. He was Johnny Bench's backup for a few years with the Reds.

One of the top pitchers in Hawaii in 1973 and 1974 was Ed Acosta. I had faced Acosta in 1970 when I was with Tidewater and he was with Columbus, the Pirates' affiliate. When I faced him for the first time, he drilled me in my right hip. In the same game, Danny Rivas, a lefty pitcher, drilled me in my left hip. I guess those two Latin ballplayers didn't like me. So I saw Acosta in Hawaii and asked him why he had hit me. He told me it was because I was leading the league in hitting. He was a hot-tempered guy who had been an amateur boxer. Ed was a big strong, tough guy. Years later, I had him throw batting practice to my Little League team and he could still throw. My kids were scared to death of him. He would still throw inside to these young kids. I said, "Ed, just let them hit the ball." He got on that mound and he was a tiger. He was menacing, not just to me but to my kids. Ed loves the game of baseball and still works with kids. Can you imagine, I'm leading the league in hitting and he's never seen me before, and he drills me?

I got called up to the Padres in May. I don't know why they called me up when they hardly played me. I got into 33 games in two months, always coming off the bench. I hit .214 with one RBI. It's tough when you're going back and forth. I hit .278 with two homers and 20 RBI in Hawaii. John McNamara was the Padres manager. I didn't talk to him much and he didn't talk to me. Maybe I would've liked him more if I was starting. But he was alright. He managed six different teams, and Mets fans remember him as the Red Sox manager in 1986.

One of the games I played in was at Shea Stadium. I went into the game as a pinch-runner. From first base I was looking in the dugout and Seaver was looking at me. I don't know why, because I never talked to him before or after the game. I ended up making the last out of that game with the bases loaded and the Mets leading by a run.

Willie McCovey was on the Padres in 1974. The team had traded my minor league teammate Mike Caldwell to the Giants. Caldwell would pitch well for the Brewers later on in his career. McCovey stayed to himself. I don't remember him talking to anybody. He was always off by himself. He was quite a loner. I didn't talk to him once.

A young Dave Winfield was also on the club. He was drafted in a few sports out of Minnesota. The Padres picked him, as well as teams in the NBA and ABA. And the Vikings picked him, even though Winfield had never played college football. Obviously he picked the right sport. He didn't even play in the minors. He was a great athlete. The guy could run, throw, and hit. He had a rocket for an arm. There was one time he caught a ball in right field with a man on third base tagging up and Derrel Thomas, playing second base, was in short right field. Winfield cut loose with a rocket and Derrel was in the line of Dave's throw. As soon as Winfield let it go, Thomas went to the ground because he saw the ball coming at him. He drilled Thomas. I think it's the funniest thing I have ever seen on a baseball field. People were cracking up although I don't think Thomas thought it was funny.

Fred Kendall was the catcher. His son, Jason, had a good career in the majors. Jim McAndrew was on that Padres team. It was his last year in the majors. He had a good career as a control pitcher. Decades later we were at Mets fantasy camp and we had the final game against the campers, and Jim, in his middle 60s, could still throw. Randy Jones lost 22 games for San Diego, two years later he won 22 and the Cy Young. He recently beat throat cancer.

Dave Roberts, the number one pick in 1972, was one of my favorite guys I ever met in baseball. Like Winfield, he went from college to the big leagues also. He worked very hard. He would play any position that they wanted him to play. He became a good catcher in addition to being an infielder, although he didn't have the career that you think a number one overall pick would have. It's hard to say why. He had the tools.

You just don't know with the draft. Dave Roberts was picked number one overall while Dennis Eckersley and Gary Carter were picked later in that draft. Mike Piazza had to be picked as a favor and he ends up in the Hall of Fame. I have a friend, John Flannery, who went to Lakewood High School after I did and played pro ball. John was an infielder who played a few games for the 1977 White Sox. He's a scout now and he told me drafting players is a crapshoot. They go by what they see on the field and they talk to the kid, and they talk to his family. Even the pro scouts don't know all the time. Dave Roberts had a good career. How many guys make it to the majors, let alone stick around? Now he's doing some scouting. A lot of these guys love the game and find a way to stay in it.

In 1975, we had Bill Almon in Hawaii. He was a number one overall pick. I remember seeing him when I was with the Padres and he had just signed, and they brought him to the team to work out although he didn't play until September. Almon was taking batting practice and throwing, and Cito Gaston looked at me and said, "This is the number one pick?" The way he swung the bat wasn't impressive at all.

Bill played less than 40 games in the minors before he made his debut with the Padres although he was back in the minors the next year. Between him and Winfield skipping the minors, they didn't waste much time. The Padres probably didn't have anybody else who could play, so they had to bring them up and make them face the fire real fast.

The first year in Hawaii Almon didn't hit much but he was aggressive, a good fielder, and he was a hard worker. Almon was a smart kid who went to Brown. And he made himself a very good ballplayer who spent 15 seasons in the majors. He never had that much physical talent but did it with hard work. In his two seasons in Hawaii he hit .228 and then .291, so you could see the progression. He even hit .300 one year for the White Sox.

Jerry Turner could hit. He would always tear into Hartsfield. He'd always talk about him. I don't know why because Hartsfield always played him a lot. Who knows why any of us say anything? It's called gossip.

We had Gus Gil, who had been an infielder with the Seattle Pilots. Sonny Jackson, who stole 49 bases for Houston one year, was with us. He wasn't much of a hitter but a good defensive player. Steve Huntz was a good switch-hitting infielder who hit 12 home runs for the Hawaii Islanders.

Gary Ross led the team with 16 wins. He was a good thrower. Butch Metzger won 15. Chuck Hartenstein pitched well for us. Jerry Johnson won 10 games for us. He was a teammate of mine when I was in Williamsport. We called him "Neck" because he had a big neck. Brent Strom was a good lefty pitcher who is now, in my opinion, the best pitching coach in Major League Baseball with the Houston Astros. Brent and I had been on the California Collegiate League team that played at Dodger Stadium almost 10 years earlier.

I was a fan favorite in Hawaii. One paper did an article about me called "Rocket Rod." That name stuck. Even today, guys call me Rocket. I was the Rocket before Roger Clemens was. The fans were great and always good to me. They were very supportive of the team and I don't remember them ever booing. Sometimes they would throw money on the field if a guy hit a home run. I know they never threw me any money. Hawaii is a very sports-minded island.

 A day in Hawaii for me was, I'd wake up, go to the beach, go home, have something to eat, take a nap, and then go to the ballpark. That's not a bad life. We played well in Hawaii. Opponents who came from Phoenix, or wherever they were on the coast, didn't get much sleep when they came to play us. It was a big advantage. We'd have homestands that lasted three weeks and then we'd have a three-week road trip.

We also had these jerseys which are kind of like the Astros "Tequila Sunrise" jerseys from the '80s. We didn't really care though. We'd wear whatever they wanted us to wear.

George Brunet was a left-handed pitcher who played for nine different teams in the big leagues and eventually went to Mexico and made the Mexican Baseball Hall of Fame. George was famous for wearing no underwear when he was playing. What a character. Good pitcher though.

There was catcher Merritt Ranew, who had been on the expansion Houston Colt .45s and expansion Seattle Pilots.

Third baseman John Werhas was another popular guy in Hawaii. He was an excellent athlete at USC and was drafted by the Lakers but chose to sign with the Dodgers instead. Werhas played a bit for the Dodgers and he told me how Sandy Koufax would hang around the younger players and how they looked up to him. John did well in Hawaii and had his own sports program. One day he was in an elevator and some guy was talking to him about the LORD and Werhas got to thinking about it. John became a pastor and would lead baseball chapel services for Major League Baseball. He eventually opened a church in Southern California.

Mickey Mantle came to Hawaii for a home run exhibition. The poor guy could barely walk, and he's up there swinging the bat, hitting balls out of the ballpark. That was another way to get fans to the stadium. The team had Clint Eastwood show up. He was one of my favorite actors. He was a good guy but you want to talk about non-athletic? Oh my goodness. He was a rugged, tough guy in the movies and he has his golf tournament at Pebble Beach. But baseball wasn't his sport. Lee Majors, The Six Million Dollar Man, came once. They would have softball games because they sure as heck couldn't play baseball. Max Patkin, the Clown Prince of Baseball, was there a few times. He was amazing. So loose and flexible with some of the things he could do with his body.

I also started using weights in the offseason. I had a guy who knew a lot about the body, and a lot about weights, Don Rowe, a former Met. He had played in the Pacific Coast League, and was a pitching coach with the Brewers. This guy was smart. He put me on a weight program, a stretching program. The last year or two that I played, I was probably in the best baseball shape of my life. I was stronger and didn't get as tired during the season. I maintained my weight throughout the year. In past years that I hadn't lifted, I would lose weight during the season.

We moved in to Aloha Stadium in 1976, which is where the NFL Pro Bowl is held each year. The stadium had artificial turf. Whoever ran the stadium told us we couldn't play on the field if we had spikes. If we had rubber cleats we could play on the field, but if anybody had spikes they were going to turn the lights off. In the bottom of the first I step into the box with my cleats on and they turned the lights off. They stopped the game and wouldn't let us play. The rubber spikes don't work on that kind of field, so eventually some kind of compromise was worked out so we could keep playing.

Bobby Valentine was with us that year. He couldn't play like he used to before an injury he suffered crashing into a wall a few years earlier but he was always a personality. People always loved Valentine. He was really popular with the fans. I probably fell to second-most popular behind him. We used to hang out on road trips.

There was a place in Tacoma away from the hotel and he would have these contests where he'd line up all these different beers. We would close our eyes, taste them, and say which one we liked best. The one that was the best was Pabst Blue Ribbon…a lot of excitement in Tacoma, you think? Valentine's brain worked a little differently than most of ours. When he managed the Mets, he once got ejected from a game and reappeared later in the dugout with a fake moustache. That's Bobby V.

Hartsfield let him manage a few games that year, which I think was Bobby's first managing experience. I think people sometimes forget how good a ballplayer he was, because he was the fifth overall pick in the draft in 1968.

There was one game, which was the second game of a doubleheader, and I was leading off the game. We were a bit short on players and Hartsfield said, "Nobody get thrown out of the game." The home plate umpire was Larry Ellis, who I didn't think was a very good at calling balls and strikes. During my first at-bat, I was disagreeing with him and he threw me out of the game, real smart move, dumb me. Your brain gets overloaded, you don't think, you just react. My dad used to say, "Don't let your mouth overload your ass." It's true. You start mouthing off and saying things you shouldn't be saying, and it catches up to you.

Joe Pepitone was in Hawaii for a while. Joe was a different guy. I usually stay away from the big-name guys but eventually we got to be friends. You talk about a flamboyant personality. Everyone liked Pepitone. He told me that when he was in New York playing first base for the Yankees, he was more popular than Mickey Mantle and Roger Maris. That's what he told me, anyway. I could see it because he was such a personality, and he could play back then.

He was with us in spring training in Yuma. Can you imagine Joe Pepitone in Yuma, Arizona, with all the cowboys? With the way he dressed and had his hair, or I should say hairpiece. He was the first ballplayer to use a blow-dryer in the clubhouse. We were probably the only ones who ever saw him without his hair. He's balder than bald and he had those beautiful rugs he used to wear. But this guy could go to a bar, already dressing louder than most New Yorkers dressed, and he could charm the people in those western bars. A guy like that with his clothes and his chains and his hairdos, and they just flocked to him. He had such a personality and they loved him. By the time he got to Hawaii he couldn't hit anymore although he could still field. He only played 13 games for the Islanders in 1976.

The guy never slept, which eventually catches up to you. There was a book out called "Joe, You Coulda Made Us Proud." I thought I've done a lot of things in life. It's nothing compared to what Pepitone's been through.

Wayne Garrett's brother, Adrian, played with us for a bit. He also played in the majors. Adrian wasn't with us in the playoffs because his dad was critically ill at the time. Mike Champion was a 21-year-old prospect and our second baseman in Hawaii. The third baseman was Dave Hilton, a hard-nosed player. He was a tiger but a very quiet guy. Gene Richards was an outfielder who hit .331 in 1976.

Diego Segui pitched for us and went on to play for the expansion Mariners in 1977. His son, David, had a good career. Eddie Watt pitched for the Islanders. He gave up the go-ahead hit to Ron Swoboda in the final game of the 1969 World Series. Eddie always had a big plug of tobacco in his cheek.

The umpires in the league were trying to get to the majors, just like the players were. One of them was Eric Gregg. If you want to see video of Gregg in action, look up the 1997 National League Championship Series and see his strike zone for Livan Hernandez against the Braves. Oh man. He struck out 15 batters and outdueled Greg Maddux, in part because pitches a foot off the plate were being called strikes. Gregg wasn't the most consistent guy. When he was an umpire in the Pacific Coast League, I heard a story that Gregg would get physically sick before umpiring behind home plate. Sadly, he passed away a number of years ago. He had some weight issues that caused health problems. That was back when there was an issue with a lot of umpires being overweight, which included, tragically, John McSherry dying on the field on Opening Day in Cincinnati.

We had to win the last game of the regular season in Hawaii just to tie for our division. And we won it to stay alive. When we went on road trips, we would usually fly out the night the Hawaii homestand ended. So we flew all night to Tacoma, for a one-game playoff for the division title. We get there in the morning and I hadn't slept all night. I never did sleep well on airplanes. In that game I led off with a triple off the left field fence off of a pitcher I hadn't hit all year. Bobby Valentine came up next and hit a sacrifice fly and I scored. We won the game 2-0. Now we headed to Salt Lake City to play the Angels' farm club for the Pacific Coast League Championship. We get there in the morning and again I hadn't slept. After playing the night before, flying out, and then playing again, we won the first game of the series. I led off and got three hits off Wayne Simpson after getting no rest. And one of the hits was with the game tied in the ninth inning. I finally get some sleep and I'm feeling good the next day, and we lose. That shows you how baseball can be. I was fully rested and went hitless in four at-bats. Sometimes when you're tired you play better, maybe because you're more relaxed. We went on to win the series. Their left fielder, Frankie George, had a critical drop in a game when he tried making a one-handed catch.

All the playoff games had to be played in Salt Lake City. Jack Quinn, general manager and president of the Islanders, was dealing with financial restraints and didn't have money to fly the team back and forth. A lot of times, the team was late sending checks to Hawaii players. I didn't have to worry about that because I was still owned by the Padres so I always got paid. Quinn was trying hard to keep the team going but that was one reason we didn't have a home-and-away series with Salt Lake City.

It was nice winning another championship, and I was named to the All-Star team that season. I was always an All-Star in the minor leagues if I got to play a full season. There wasn't actually an All-Star Game, but a group of players named as All-Stars in the league with me as the center fielder. Carlos Lopez, who played with a few teams in the late '70s, was the left fielder. Jack Clark, who would go on to be a four-time All-Star, was the right fielder. The first baseman was Doug Ault, who later hit the first home run in Blue Jays history. At second base was Bump Wills, the son of Maury, who would play a few seasons with the Rangers. At shortstop was Johnnie LeMaster, who would play 10 seasons with the Giants. Wayne Gross, who would be an All-Star with Oakland, was at third. Behind the plate was Gary Alexander, who played for four teams in seven seasons. The designated hitter was Bob Gorinski, who played one season with the Twins. Mark Wiley was the right-handed pitcher. He later got into coaching and has had a long career doing that. The left-handed pitcher was Bob Knepper, who was a two-time All-Star and part of the 1986 Astros rotation with Nolan Ryan and Mike Scott that won a division title.

Of all the players named to that All-Star team, I was the only one who didn't play in the majors after 1976.

A few months after winning the 1976 PCL title, the expansion draft for the Blue Jays and Seattle Mariners was held. Bavasi's son, Peter, became the general manager in Toronto and he hired Roy Hartsfield to be the first manager for the Blue Jays. I figured at age 30, if I was going to get back to the big leagues that's where it would be, because I had played for Hartsfield and had good years for him. Instead they drafted a lot of younger kids, and that's when I decided to retire and get out of the game. It would've been interesting to see the American League parks like Yankee Stadium and Fenway Park, and going to cities I had never been to before.

I probably could've played another five years but I didn't know if I'd go back to the majors. So I said goodbye. Adios. The Padres sent me a contract for 1977 that I was looking at the other day. It was for a big, whopping $2,400 a month. I told Mike Port, the minor league administrator for the Padres, and later general manager of the Angels, that I wasn't coming back. He said he figured I wouldn't.

It's tough to keep playing at age 30 and up if you don't know you're going to get back to the Major Leagues unless you're just a baseball lifer, which some guys are. I didn't want to do it. I got tired of the traveling. And I never really missed it. Some guys want to stay in however they can. God bless them for it. But it was time for me to get out and do something else.

Over the years I kept wondering why Hartsfield didn't draft me. They took one kid, Gary Woods, who was seven years younger than me. He hit .216 and was sent back down to the minors. There were other outfielders who were picked over me, to my surprise. The only thing I could think of was that they were younger than I was. Al Woods, Gary Woods, Otto Velez, John Scott and Steve Bowling were the main outfielders Toronto used that season, and none of them were over 26 years old. The only real veteran they used as a position player was Ron Fairly, who was in his 20th season in the majors and actually made the All-Star team.

Years later I called Roy, just to say hello and see how he was doing. Even before I said anything, he goes, "Rodney, I wanted to draft you, and have you lead off and play centerfield in 1977, but I couldn't draft you." I asked what he meant that he couldn't draft me. Roy said, "Toronto was an American League ball club and the Padres were a National League club and we were only allowed to draft guys from American League ballclubs."

I didn't think anything of it at the time. OK, that sounds reasonable. But later on I'm thinking, if he wanted me so much, why didn't he trade for me? So I wondered if Roy told me one thing but still he could have got me if he wanted me that badly. The Blue Jays actually purchased the contracts of Dave Hilton, Dave Roberts and John Scott from the Padres. Wait a second, something isn't right here. If they wanted me badly enough, they could have acquired me. Apparently they'd rather have those other guys than me and I had a better season in 1976 than all of those guys.

But they didn't want me, which is fine. I don't hold grudges or have any bad feelings. I have no complaints. God has blessed me. You always want to be told the truth. Just be honest, even if it hurts. A lot of times, the truth hurts.

No need to be upset about the past, just learn from it. So I proceeded on with my life from that point. I knew he had a guilty conscience if he brought it up as I'm saying hi to him.

Right away he went into it that he couldn't draft me, which seemed weird to me.

Roy was a good man who lasted three years in Toronto. They lost at least 100 games in each of those first three seasons. As a competitor, it means I missed out on a lot of losing, although I still would have liked to have been there. Nobody likes to lose, but if you're going to lose, at least it's in the big leagues.

They wouldn't win a World Series until 1992, when Cito Gaston was the manager. I had played in San Diego with Cito. I remember sitting on the bench with him and Nate Colbert and they were really funny.

Life After Baseball

Very few guys get to go out on their own terms like Derek Jeter or Chipper Jones. But I did go out on my own terms. I wasn't released by San Diego. I decided to walk away.

I played pro ball for 10 years, which is longer than most people, but what am I going to do with the next 40 or 50 years on this earth? If you don't handle your finances correctly, which most people don't, you're going to be hurting down the road. All you have to do is look at a guy's lifestyle to tell what's going to happen down the road. Mike Tyson is a good example. How do you blow half a billion dollars? How does that happen? He was involved with the wrong people and his wild lifestyle got him in trouble.

When I said I was done, Sheridan was shocked at first. She enjoyed the baseball season. It kind of surprised my dad also because he thought I should keep playing. I thought I could play another five years if I wanted. I was in shape and could still run, throw and field. But I said, "No. I'm done."

It was kind of funny that I played baseball all my life, and after I got out, I never missed the game. Never.

I ran into this so-called friend of mine, a former ballplayer, who years before had gotten me to invest in commodities. This "friend of mine" got me involved with this company called Goldstein, Samuelson Inc., which sold commodities for the futures market. Eventually Goldstein was thrown in jail for running a corrupt operation. Years later, he got out and he was doing the same thing and got indicted again. What did I know about money at that time? So I put in about $10,000. I ended up losing the money. At the time I was devastated because $10,000 was a lot then. It's a lot now. So I had to start going to work for a living. Thankfully I lost it at a young age where I could still work and make it back.

Anyway, I meet up with this ballplayer on my way home just to see him and make amends. I go to his house and he's not there, which didn't surprise me. His wife and child were there. So the guy comes home and he was happy because he had sold an IRA to some guy. He had been out of the game a few years and got into the insurance business. He's mouthing off and cocky. I asked how he was doing. I was being nice and cordial.

I'm there a while, and eventually he ended up making some derogatory comments and that ticked me off. I threw a left and knocked him down. I drilled the sucker with a left. He didn't know what hit him. His wife had no reaction. She probably knew he deserved it. I apologized to his wife. I left and was walking out to my car and he runs outside with a bat in his hands. And I said, "You want some more of this?" He just sat down on the fender of his car and started crying. Can you imagine that? A supposedly tough ballplayer was crying? I don't know if he was crying from being hit or he was embarrassed because the incident happened in front of his wife and kid…probably the latter.

I was working for my dad in the ironwork business in the offseason and I started to like it. I looked around and saw some of these 40-year-old guys all hunched over. I said, "I don't think so." I went from a big high in being a World Series champion who was traveling all over the world to a big low in working labor. For most people that is not a low because

149

you're supposed to work and do a regular job. But I wasn't used to that. I was a spoiled ex-baseball player.

It's nice that I had a great wife who hung in there with me unlike a lot of wives of professional athletes. Being a mother and a housewife is probably the toughest job there is for a woman. We decided we didn't want her working outside the house, although at one point, Sheridan got her real estate license and made a few sales. I didn't like being home watching the kids. I mean, I love my kids, but I don't want to be home while my wife is out working. I'm not a Mr. Mom type of guy.

In November, my wife and I went to dinner at this Mexican restaurant. I recognized a relief pitcher for Salt Lake City, John Verhoeven. He was a big guy who was a submarine pitcher. I went over and said, "Hey John, I'm Rod Gaspar, I played ball against you." He looks up at me and goes, "Oh yeah. I remember you when I was a kid." I didn't know his personality at the time, but I later learned he was kidding.

I got to know John and his wife Kathy. About two weeks later, Kathy calls me and asks if I want to go down to her office and interview for a job. I asked what she did and she told me she sold life insurance...life insurance? OK. I'll listen to anything or anybody.

I met with a man named Dick Pohlman. I'm 30 years old and I've been a baseball guy my whole life. I walk into his office and I'm wearing a long sleeve shirt with the shirt tail out, slacks, and sandals. Great appearance for a job interview, right? All I knew how to do was throw a ball, catch a ball, hit a ball.
This guy did a sales job on me and I ended up selling life insurance. I came home to Sheridan and said, "Well, one of

us is quitting our job and it's not going to be me." We wanted her at home with the kids.

I didn't know anything about money. You get in that business, you start learning real fast. After a while in the business, I realized that losing that $10,000 in the early 70s was one of the best things to ever happen to me financially, because it made me realize that life isn't about being a baseball player. That's living a fantasy, thinking you're going to play ball your whole life. Losing $10,000 taught me a big lesson about money. You need to earn your money. In this great opportunistic country you can have your ups and downs, but if you never give up and never give in, you can be successful.

Never give up, never give in. That's one of my mottos in life.

One idea I've picked up in business is that 10 percent of the people own 90 percent of the wealth, and 90 percent of the people own 10 percent of the wealth. And the 90 percent of the people end up working for the other 10 percent for their whole lives.

My first client was my dad. He said, "I want to buy a life insurance policy." I said, "OK. Let me explain how it works, dad." Typical of my dad, he goes, "I don't want to hear your bullshit." I said, "OK."

The second policy I sold was to Tony Muser, who played with me at Lakewood High School and later went on to manage the Royals. I told Muser what I was doing and he laughed at me. "You're doing what?" And he ended up buying a policy from me and I was on my way.

I started working at this office in Santa Ana in November 1976. There were a few former ballplayers selling insurance at the time. They would have Bible study, and they asked me to attend one. I said, "What's a Bible study?" I didn't know what a Bible was, let alone a Bible study. I had never really gone to church. I started attending their meetings on Friday mornings at eight.

I was attending for a month, and then Christmas Day I went upstairs and asked Jesus Christ into my life and heart as my Lord and Savior. I became a Christian. I didn't even tell my wife immediately. Eventually I did, and we started going to church.

After a month, the pastor called me. The pastor, Jim Folkers, came to the house and we spoke some, talking about the Bible and GOD. He asked me if I had accepted Jesus Christ into my life, and I told him I had. He asked Sheridan if she had. She said she always believed in GOD but had never let the LORD in her heart. The pastor asked if she would like to, and she did. We started basically living a new life, going to church, taking the kids to church, raising our kids in the Christian faith.

People always wanted me to make appearances because of my time with the Mets. It got around that Rod Gaspar lived in Mission Viejo and he played on the 1969 Mets, and he's a Christian so maybe he'll speak at our Bible study. For a number of years I would make appearances at churches and functions, and tell them about my background. It's called a testimony. That was one of the offshoots of becoming Christian, becoming a public speaker. I enjoyed it. Playing baseball, you get exposed to a lot of situations, a lot of people, so crowds really don't bother you.

Sure, I'd go speak and be a little nervous at the start, but once I started it didn't make a difference if it's 10 people there or 200 people. You're talking about something you know, and it's your life. You express the words and hope people are encouraged by what you're saying.

I wasn't surprised that I didn't miss baseball. There are guys, like Tony Muser, who stay in the game as coaches because they probably loved it more than I did. Those guys stay in the minors for years coaching, or doing whatever they do. They pay their dues big time. I think that's wonderful that they have the tenacity to hang in there. I didn't want to travel anymore, so I never really missed it. I liked being at home. A lot of these guys, like me, didn't really have anything to fall back on. There wasn't a job waiting for m., I wasn't making the money the players are making now, where if they do the right thing they can be set for life.

But a lot of guys don't do the right thing. Whether it's baseball, football, boxing, it doesn't matter. Mike Tyson lost hundreds of millions of dollars. Just look at their lifestyles. That's all you have to do. I made a list of athletes who went broke. And I mean recent ones, not guys in my day who had to work in the offseason. Look at Lenny Dykstra and Darryl Strawberry and Dwight Gooden. Strawberry seems to be doing well now. But you can't live a crazy lifestyle without it catching up to you.

It's like how getting to the majors is tough, but staying is even tougher. It's one thing to make money, and another thing to keep it.

For the first three months I was in the insurance business, they gave a bonus which was a hook to keep me in. To me, it's the toughest business as far as selling is concerned. You're selling the intangible. You can't eat it, you can't live in it, you can't drive it. You're selling death, and people don't want to talk about death. I've got to convince them that I'm selling life. That's why the commissions are good compared to what most people sell.

We're all in the selling business. I'm in the selling business, you're in the selling business, we're all in the selling business in this country. We're all selling something.

After four months of selling insurance, I had made $20,000. That was more than I made in any one season in baseball. I thought that if I made $20,000 every year, man, I'd be making a lot of money. To me, it was a lot of money and it helped us out big time. But it fluctuates and there were years where I didn't make any money. It wasn't all roses. We had our ups and downs.

It got to a point in the early '80s where we maxed out two credit cards, both of them at $5,000. We also had a second mortgage on the house. And I'm in the business of trying to help people save money? I'm the biggest hypocrite insurance guy out there. I'm trying to help people save money and I'm in debt. What kind of an insurance guy am I?

And we had more kids. Corte was born in 1979, and David Matthew was born in 1982.

At that time it was pretty easy to get into a house and we moved to Virginia. We had been married in Tidewater, although that's not where we lived. We bought a home outside Richmond. I don't know why we picked that area. I have no idea. I had gotten tired of Southern California. My wife was ready to move, too. So we sold the house, packed up and left. We made about $90,000 on the house in California. At the time, interest rates were real high. We were putting money into these accounts and making about 18 percent on them.

In Virginia, we bought a home which we really liked. But we hated it there. That was another learning experience that helped me get fired up about working. Because when I was in Virginia, we didn't make any money. We almost went through that $90,000. Another stupid financial move on Gaspar's part, thinking moving was the best scenario but actually we were running away from California for some inexplicable reason.

Virginia wasn't the same and we realized we missed California. We were only there for about 11 months. I had very few appointments and I was bored. It wasn't a good time. We sold the house for a little less than we paid for it, but I didn't care.

When I went back to California to look for a house, I decided to drive back and tried to do it in 50 hours. I was having a game with myself to drive from Virginia to California without stopping. That's over 2,500 miles in a 1971 Vista Cruiser station wagon. (I kept that car into the early '90s.) I dozed off a little in Texas. I pulled over to rest a few times but never went to a hotel or anything. I got to Arizona and went to a Mexican restaurant. So I had some food and about an hour later, I had to pull over at a rest stop and go to sleep. I couldn't quite make it. After I woke up, I started driving for a bit and then had to pull over again because I was still tired. Eventually I made it to California, but it took me 53 or 54 hours. I couldn't do it in 50 hours.

I found a nice place, and then took a flight back to Virginia. I was the last one on the plane, and I was the first one off the plane. As I went out to the front of the airport, Sheridan had just pulled up in the other car we had, an Isuzu. She picked me up and we went back home. And within a day or two somebody bought our home in Virginia. The timing for everything was perfect...thank you, LORD.

On the day we were leaving, it was snowing heavily but I couldn't wait. It could've been all kinds of bad weather but I didn't care. We're out of here. So I drove in the snow and we were on our way back to California. It was Sheridan and I and the three kids. And Sheridan was pregnant with David. We drove cross country, although this time we made a number of stops because we had the kids.

Back in Mission Viejo, we got into our home. It was a nice four-bedroom place for $165,000. We didn't even have to qualify to get into the house. I assumed the loans. There's a difference. If you qualify for a loan, you have to have the income to back it up. Back then, you could assume a loan without telling them what you made. I wasn't making much money and that was the only way we were going to get into a house, but I was in over my head, barely making monthly payments and having two credit cards maxed out.

Doug Sanders, the old golfer, once said, "I'm working as hard as I can to get my life and my cash to run out at the same time. If I die after lunch Tuesday, everything will be perfect." I think a lot of guys feel that way.

There is some statistic that says 90 percent of people who start a new business will fail in the first year of the business. And of the remaining 10 percent, 70 percent of them will fail in the second year. It's a long shot, especially selling insurance. But my attitude was, hey, I got to the big leagues. I signed a professional contract. Very few people do that. I played well in the minor leagues; very few people do that. I got to the big leagues. Very few people do that. And thankfully I was in the World Series. Very few people do that. So I figured if I can get to the major leagues in baseball, I can do anything. And that's my attitude today. Never give up, never give in.

Even though we were, in a sense, broke, I just kept plugging away. I give all the credit to GOD. I really do. I had no prospects out there, and He kept providing the people for me to talk to. Nobody is going to just give you money. You have to go out and earn it. Eventually I got more and more successful in the business.

I'm not a kind of guy to bug people. I never did cold calls. I didn't feel comfortable doing that. I didn't like people cold-calling and bugging me. To this day I don't. I felt bad bugging people, but I had to because I had to make a living to take care of my family. Thankfully I was in this business, which is a great business. It's the best business I could be in for me. It gave me time to be with my family and work with my kids in sports. For a guy who didn't like bugging people, I ended up being a pretty successful guy.

I took an insurance test one time, and I answered all the questions, truthfully of course. And it comes back that I would be a terrible salesman. And it was because I would be honest. I wouldn't answer questions a certain way. I was very direct. I was probably in the top 10 percent of insurance salesmen in this country during my career. In baseball, I was in the top one percent. Gee, I guess I was a better ballplayer than a life insurance salesman.

I have my own insurance business. I still have my clients and talk to them, but I don't pursue the business like I used to. One thing I learned, which is the key to financial success, as far as I'm concerned, is have no debt. Ninety-five percent of people age 65 have debt. They have a hard time retiring. You can't have any debt, especially when you're older. You have to pay off your house, pay off your car. I learned that lesson when I maxed out those credit cards at $5,000 each. After we came out of that fiasco, we worked to get out of debt and we basically have one credit card which we pay off every month. That's what I suggest. You don't want that to accumulate over the years.

The problem today is people spend more than they make. I've been in the financial business for 42+ years. Most people are almost broke by the time they get to retirement age because they haven't saved any money. A lot of people are in that position. If you put away 10 percent of your money every year, you won't have to worry about it and depend on the government. Pay your taxes, pay your bills and you'll be fine. Don't live over your head like I did, and a majority of people in this country do.

I know people in California who have $5,000 per month house payments and almost $20,000 in property taxes per year because they want to live how everyone else lives. Well you can't live that way unless you have the money. It takes a number of years to earn that money.

Taylor Gaspar was born in 1986. So the first child was a girl, followed by three boys in the middle, and one more girl. When people ask me how many kids I have, I get the funniest reactions when I say I have five. "Five kids? What are you, a Mormon or a Catholic?" I tell them I'm a Christian, but I guess most people don't have more than three kids, and a lot of them just have two.

We raised the kids in Mission Viejo. They were good kids, and still are to this day. And my grandkids are great. My kids never got involved in things like parties, drinking, smoking, drugs. I can't complain.

Jokingly, I would say, "Is Little League for the parents and not for the kids?" Parents get so involved and there are so many horror stories about parents in Little League. Obviously it's for the kids, but you hear parents saying things and doing things. The Little League board would change the rules on draft night against me. You're picking the order of boys on your team, and they would change the order so that I would draft last. I would still end up winning most of the time. I don't know why they did that. Maybe because I was a former major league ballplayer and they tried to make it harder for me to win. It didn't work. We won anyway.

In coaching Little League from 1982 through 1991, I only had a problem with one dad. If you got him away from the Little League field he was nice guy, but he wasn't real nice about the games. His boy was the best player on the team. I got along well with the kid, as I did with all my players. There was one game where the dad yelled something from the stands at me, and I went over and told him to zip it. This was in front of everybody. In a way, I felt bad for him. He was a successful guy in business with great kids, and a nice wife. I guess his wife got tired of him too, because years later I found out she divorced the guy. She couldn't put up with him. The boy became a very good basketball player and received a college scholarship.

One year, I'm coaching our second son, Corte, and that kid is on the mound in the championship game. He wasn't pitching well and we were behind 3-1. He comes in from the mound and I grab him by the jersey, brought him into the dugout and I verbally (no cussing) hammered him. I should have waited until he came in the dugout because we were in full view of the crowd.

After that talk, he settled down and pitched better, and we won the championship. Of course, I got a call from the president of the Little League, telling me I can't grab a kid like that. They wanted to make a big deal of it but I blew it off. Some kids need to be kicked (not physically) in the butt to motivate them. Others don't.

There was one time that I was coaching third base during a game, and the opposing pitcher was getting wild. I yelled to my kids, "Take a pitch.He's not throwing strikes." I don't know if it was the nicest thing to do because maybe it got in his head. He was a nice kid. His father was watching and goes, "That Gaspar is a son of a bitch." Turns out my dad was near him and heard it. My dad goes up to this guy despite being about 30 years older, and probably being outweighed by 40 pounds. The guy started to leave and my dad goes after him and followed him out of the ballpark, threatening to kick his butt. That's how my dad was. You didn't go after his kids. He told me after the game, "Man, I'm hot." I thought he meant because of the sun, because it was a hot day. I asked if he was fine. He goes, "Oh yeah, I'm fine. It's just that son of a bitch called you a son of a bitch."

I would draft nice parents as opposed to drafting talented kids, who I thought could be problems, because I didn't want any issues. So I'm coaching Doug Harrison. His dad, Mike, and I grew up together. Doug did a lot of talking and would get on my nerves sometimes. I would get on him a bit but he was a good kid and he would take it. It didn't faze him one way or the other and he did a good job for us on the field. One day we were taking batting practice before the game. (I think I was the first coach to have pre-game batting practice before Little League games. This was before everyone was doing it.) So I guess I yelled at Doug. We're walking to the main field to get ready for the game and Doug's parents are by the gate we're going to walk in. Doug walks in front of me, sees his parents and says, "Well, Mr. Gaspar yelled at me again." He told his parents when I was right there. Doug didn't care. I look over at his parents and they are smiling. They didn't say a word.

I also caused controversy after the 1988 championship games. I was coaching Cade, who was 15. And I was coaching Corte, who was nine. I was coaching both teams as they were in different divisions. Both teams got to their respective championship games, and both teams ended up losing. So they have the final ceremony, and they call on the managers to say nice, wonderful things about the kids. So I went up there and congratulated the two other teams for playing well and winning. I said, "My kids on my team are not losers. They're winners in my book. You show me a good loser and I'll show you a loser."

It was an old quote (from Leo Durocher), and it was true in my book. You can't be a good loser. You can have class in losing, but if you're laughing and all that, it's different. I see football and basketball players lose a game and congratulate the other team. I don't understand that.

So I made that comment and people went crazy. People were sending letters to the Little League board. "Gaspar is a loser." I kept a letter from this couple who had a kid on one of the winning teams. They were irate and wrote a letter to the league president. The wife was the one who wrote it because her husband was the kind of guy that walked around with a purse. They carry those little bags that look like purses. A couple of years ago, I got to thinking about that letter and decided to call these people and apologize. So I get on the phone and reach them. I tell them I'm Rod Gaspar from Little League way back when and I wanted to apologize for making some of the comments I did. They didn't remember it. They had completely forgotten about it.

I knew someone who wanted me to coach baseball at Trabuco Hills High School in Mission Viejo. He had gone to Lakewood High School a few years before me and became the principal at Trabuco Hills and he asked me if I would be interested in coaching the team. Another friend of mine was the athletic director at Saddleback Junior College, and he mentioned that baseball coaching job to me. But I couldn't get out of the insurance business because I had a family to support. Those coaching jobs take up so much of your time. So I declined the jobs, not that they formally asked me anyway. I've thought about getting into coaching past the Little League level, but never did it. I think I could've done a good job. Especially at Saddleback, because they had so many good players over the years that I like to think that I could have won a few state titles.

I coached my kids in Little League. Our youngest son, David, was a good-looking, smart kid. I can look back and say now that he was our most all-around talented child. In 1991, I was the coach of the Major Dodgers Little League team. It was a regular team with 11- and 12-year-olds, but I put David on the team. He was only eight and turned nine during the season. But he was such a good athlete. He was eight and playing against kids that were 12. He actually played centerfield for us a couple of times.

There was a tournament where we were playing against a team from Newport Beach. They had a pitcher who was about 5' 10" and I told David to hang in there against him. I knew the father of the pitcher because he was a fellow handball player. I was talking to my team in the dugout before the game and the dad came in the dugout to say hi to me. I wasn't real nice to him. I said I was talking to my kids and that I'd talk to him later. I think I ticked him off, which I'm not real proud of. But as a coach, I get as involved in the game as I did as a player. My little David got a base hit off this big pitcher, which led to us winning. That was one of the last games he ever played.

162

In early 1992, he was diagnosed with leukemia. He wasn't doing well so we took him to a doctor, who had been the doctor for the child of a family friend who had cancer. This was the only doctor we knew who dealt with childhood cancer. We didn't know anything. She misdiagnosed the cancer and gave him chemotherapy, which she shouldn't have done. He almost died from that. She told us we had to get David out of the local hospital in Santa Ana. They came and airlifted him to UCLA Medical Center.

We didn't know why he was bruising. The doctor was treating him and David started bleeding internally. He was basically out of it for two months with tubes down his throat.

He passed away in April. It was April 10, 1992, although the gravestone says April 11. It was tragic. I think about what our poor boy went through. He was so tough. He should've died early on but he was a fighter. He should've died one week after getting that terrible disease that was misdiagnosed but he lasted two and a half months. David is waiting for us in Heaven now.

People can't relate to it. They try to say things about it, but you can't say anything. You have to keep your mouth shut. You can't say, "Well, I know how you feel." No, you don't. I've had run-ins with people who told me they know how I feel. Bullshit. You don't know how I feel. You don't know how anybody who loses a child feels. To me, losing your own child is worse than losing a spouse, your parents, or anything, by far. I think Sheridan feels the same way. It's your own flesh and blood. Especially when they are so young. You don't want to lose a child no matter what, but at least if he was a bit older, at least they would have had some kind of a life. But a nine-year-old kid, my goodness. It's not fair, but life is not fair, as we know. We're not promised anything.

David had been at UCLA Medical Center, and the bill was well over $1 million. Our insurance covered some of it but not all of it. I had collection agencies calling me at night while we were trying to eat dinner. I would just go off on those assholes. I'd be cussing at them and telling them not to ever call me again. My kids and wife were sitting there while I'm hammering these people over the phone. This is after our boy dies. What kind of scumbags would call you after your boy died and ask you for money? Give me a break. And we had been great on credit, never late on anything, always paying our bills, no debt to speak of. I had a friend who was an attorney and he told me that he might be able to help. He negotiated with UCLA and whoever else he dealt with and I ended up paying less than $10,000. That satisfied the people at UCLA because we haven't heard from them since.

It was tough. Cade, our oldest son, quit playing baseball for that season because his mind wasn't into it. After David passed away, I wouldn't really allow the kids to talk about him. I put all the pictures of him away. It was devastating. I handled it so poorly. Of course, now I see how tough it was on the kids and their dad was acting like a jerk on top of it. To this day, I regret how I handled it. I didn't grieve properly. I didn't know how to grieve anyway. I still don't.

I wasn't a good dad at that time and I wasn't in a good mood, obviously. I'm still not. I'm still pissed off about it, but what are you going to do? I softened over the years. We have pictures of David everywhere. He's still constantly on my mind, and Sheridan's mind, and the kids' minds. My grandkids play baseball and wear number 3, which was David's number. Recently, I went to see my youngest grandson, Cade's son, play soccer, and he was wearing number 3.

Sheridan and I are Christians, and a tragedy can push you one of two ways with GOD. You can either renounce Him or get closer to Him. Thankfully, we got closer to GOD because we know that's our only hope to see David again. Sure, I cursed GOD when it happened. I wasn't happy and I had a short fuse. But you need to get closer to Him after something like that. There's no way to get through this without faith in GOD. If you're out there on your own, trying to beat it on your own, you're going to drive yourself nuts. I'm telling you, you'll go crazy, thinking, What could I have done? What should I have done to keep my boy alive? Why did I do this? Why didn't I do that earlier on? Why didn't I see this coming? You can go nuts over this. It's good to have faith in GOD and knowing that you will see your kid again. If you're not a believer, if you don't believe in GOD, and you lose a mom or dad or sister or brother or wife, then there's no hope for you to ever see them again. Sheridan and I know we will see our boy again. It keeps us going. It's been over 26 years since we lost him, and it doesn't get easier. It will just hit you out of nowhere. The other day my wife and I were breaking down in tears.

Like I said, I wasn't in the best of moods in 1992 or thereafter. In November of that year, our Church, Grace Community, had a softball team and they needed another player and asked me if I would play. I said, "No. I don't want to play. I know if I play I can get real fired up and I don't really want to." But the guy assured me it was pretty mild out there. The league was a city league, not a church league. It just happened that this team had guys from the church. I agreed to play first base in this night game, because I didn't want to play in the outfield. Cade was in left field.

In this particular slow-pitch softball league, the runner was allowed to take a lead off first base. So this guy gets on first base for the other team. I move in front of the first base bag, because if he leads off and I'm playing behind the bag, he cuts in front of me. If a left-handed hitter is up and they hit a line drive at me, I might have trouble seeing the ball. After the first pitch, the first-base coach says to the runner, "Run him over." I didn't pay any attention. After the next pitch, he said the same thing.

So I said, "Are you talking to him about me?"

He says, "Yeah, you're in his way."

I said, "No, I'm not. I'm right in front of the bag."

He says, "No. You're in his way."

Oh well, I blew it off.

I forgot about it. No big deal. Eventually the guy coaching first base, who was known as The Bull, comes to the plate and hits a double. The next guy singles to left, where Cade is playing. As the first baseman, I go behind home to back up the catcher. Usually in these leagues, the catcher was the worst player. So I'm backing up the catcher, and the runner scores. As The Bull is coming by me, he throws a forearm at me. Here we go again. He doesn't hit me with it but I go up to him and asked what he was doing.

So he grabs me and he starts to put me down on the ground. I started hammering him. I look at him and he's cut, and he didn't lay a hand on me. And this is happening in front of the bleachers. From 10 feet away, my wife and kids are watching the old man beat on The Bull. The Bull lost to The Matador. I am hammering this guy, and I am looking around and I am ready to go after anybody because some people are surrounding us, and I think they might be jumping me.

166

Cade comes in from left field and he's punching some guy. So we have father and son Gaspar fighting on the field with mom sitting right there. She's sitting there watching us punch guys. It was crazy. She was so ticked off.

My teammates stood around and watched. Thank you very much "teammates." Cade and I didn't get hurt, thankfully. The Bull was beat up. I hammered him. Being a Christian guy, I am not proud of this moment in my life. But a lot of anger and frustration were bottled up in the Gaspar family, Cade and myself especially...not a good time to provoke us. I remember a sermon from J. Vernon McGee, a great and well known pastor in the Christian faith. He was telling the story of a Christian and a non-Christian getting into an argument. The non-Christian knocks down the Christian. The Christian gets up and the argument continues and the Christian knocks out the non-believer. Our LORD tells us to turn the other cheek when someone hits us, but after the first time this happens, HE doesn't say in Scripture what you do the second time if the altercation continues. It is up to you what decision you make. In my case The Bull attacked me first verbally and then attacked me physically. I wasn't going to allow him to attack me again.

Afterwards, it's time for the police report. So they call me in and I tell them the story. This is the part that ticks me off. I had to pay for The Bull's' medical bills. Even though he verbally started it and physically started it, I had to pay for the medical bills. Also, because Cade came in as a third party, the league suspended him for life. I don't think he planned on playing there again anyway. I didn't play again either.
Years later, I saw Al Schmeltz, who had been a pitcher in the Mets organization. Big Al is playing in this traveling softball league. He wanted me on his team. I said I could get intense and didn't want to get too fired up on a softball field. He says,

"Rodney, those things don't happen with us." These guys were a bit older. He and his team come to the Marine base in our area, so I go watch them play. Seeing Al hit that softball was like watching a guy hit a golf ball. The ball would just rise. They're playing, and all of a sudden the catcher and pitcher start getting into it during the game. After the game, I said, "See, Al? That's why I don't play. I don't want to be involved in this stuff anymore."

Another episode happened a few months after David died. I'm driving my car and some kids started yelling at me. Now I'm still not in the best of moods. I'm on a road in Mission Viejo and I stop in the middle of the road, get out and try to reach into his car to grab this guy. Nothing happened. I didn't hit him. But the guy reported me to the police.

So I get a call and the cop has a bit of a New York accent. He asked me if I was Rod Gaspar, and I told him I was. He told me he was checking into an incident in Mission Viejo. I said that I was the guy that got out of the car and went up to this kid because he was cussing at me. The cop goes, "Are you Gaspar that played for the New York Mets?" Thank you, LORD. I got out of that one.

Sometimes that works, sometimes it doesn't. I was once leaving Biola University, and as you leave the school you head into this residential area. Biola is a Christian school in California that Todd and Tim Worrell pitched at before they made it to the majors. The speed limit was 25 and I was driving 35. I get pulled over, and as the cop is coming over I see he doesn't seem to be in a very good mood. I had my World Series ring on obviously where he could see it, and I hoped he wouldn't give me a ticket. It didn't mean a thing to that old boy. He wrote me up and said, "Don't ever speed in this area again." I said, "Yes, sir."

There was another time I was on my way to a golf tournament with Joe Moeller, a former Dodger starting pitcher in the early '60s. Joe has a huge World Series ring with the Marlins that he earned as a scout. I illegally made a turn to get out of a carpool lane. I had never done that before in my life, and a cop was right there and pulled me over. I told Moeller, "Get your ring out, Joe." He never wore his ring because it was so big, but he had it with him. The cop walks over on Joe's side. He has his ring out, and I have my ring out. The cop asked us where we were going, and Joe tells him we're going to a celebrity golf tournament. Joe and the cop are talking, and the cop ended up letting us go. So the ring helped that time. That's a $250 fine for illegally coming out of the carpool lane, so I wouldn't have been excited about paying that ticket.

It does help to have the ring, even in business. Maybe somebody finds out I played in a World Series and wants to see it. I never wore it much but Guy Baker, a business associate of mine, said that I should wear the ring for other people because how many people get to see a World Series ring? Makes sense to me.

I got to meet Mickey Mantle at an insurance seminar. He came to California while he was working for an insurance company in Texas. It was a promotional job for The Mick. He didn't actually sell insurance. Why does he have to sell insurance? He's Mickey Mantle. We went to a meeting, and there was a video showing highlights from his career and his retirement speech at Yankee Stadium. He was making comments and cracking people up. Dick Pohlmann, the man who got me into the insurance business, loved Mantle. Dick named his son Mickey, and Dick's office was on the seventh (Mantle's number) floor of his office in Santa Ana, CA.

When I met Mickey Mantle, Dick took a picture of us and in the picture I had my World Series ring on and Mickey had one of his. Mantle grabbed my hand, looked at my ring and said, "Man, Rod, that's bigger than any of the rings I've have."

That 1969 Met ring is beautiful. It's funny because Ron Swoboda never wears his ring. I've seen it and it's immaculate. It's perfect. There's no wear and tear on it at all. Our signatures are on the inside of the ring and you can still see mine but it's not as legible as Ron's.

That's what I played for. Even now, with the big money guys make, they want that ring. Not many of them get it. There aren't too many Yogi Berras out there who can win 10 as a player and then three more as a coach.

I wear my ring to card and memorabilia shows that I have attended over the years. One time I was at a card show put on by the number one promoter of card shows in the New York area, Mollie Bracigliano. I was sitting next to Bob Feller, getting ready to sign autographs. He wasn't that tall. You'd think a guy who threw that hard would be a giant. He goes, "Hey, Rod." I go, "Yes, Mr. Feller." And he says, "My hearing aid isn't working. I'm having trouble hearing." I started laughing.

Sandy Koufax was there and I got to meet him. He's not that tall either but he had the largest hands. He was a nice, pleasant man. Reggie Jackson was also there. I saw Swoboda talking to him and I went down there. I knew Reggie's reputation if he didn't know who he was talking to and he could hammer some people. There was a friend of mine, Peter Byrne, who had worked with Reggie and had developed a nice friendship with him. Before I introduced myself, I told Reggie I was a friend of Peter's. Reggie's eyes lit up and he went on about

Peter, and we had a nice conversation. I didn't mention that if he was drafted by the Mets in 1966, I probably wouldn't have been on the 1969 Mets because they would have had Reggie.

I never thought about coaching in the minors or majors. I didn't miss the game after I retired. But a few years ago I was at Mets Fantasy Camp. Sheridan and I went to Florida and had a fun time. I met a number of Mets who were younger than I, like Bernard Gilkey and Tim Teufel. There were a number of my 1969 teammates, and we had a great time.

We would have meetings every morning before we went out to the field. There was a towel rack where people throw their dirty towels and one day Lenny Randle jumped out of the rack. Lenny is something else. You're not going to meet a nicer guy. He's all over the place. I ask some of my friends what he does for a living and nobody knows. There was a special about him called "The Most Interesting Man in Baseball." He's a piece of work. He once punched his manager while playing for the Texas Rangers.

We laughed so hard watching the campers try to play baseball. You should have seen the trainers' room after the first day of games, with all these old guys just lined up outside. They had aches and pains that they never knew existed, and that was only after the first day. I had a great two weeks and thought about trying to get back in the game but I checked around and it was too late. There was no interest. It's probably better that it worked out that way.

There are guys like our catcher, Duffy Dyer, who is still in the game. Duffy played 14 seasons in the majors, and actually had an at-bat in the 1969 World Series. He's healthy and doing real well. He's still coaching in the minor leagues. He signed with the Mets in 1966, the year before I did. So he's been in the game for over 50 years. He's in great shape. He still catches and lifts weights. The baseball bug is still in him.

As a coach, I was a little strict with Cade, because I knew he had some baseball gifts. He had a really good arm, and I worked him hard as a little guy and as he got older. But he always responded. He and I were good buddies as he was growing up. When he was 13, we would throw long distance in the winter. He developed a rocket arm. As he got older, it got to the point where I would take a fungo and hit the ball as far as I could, which was about 300 plus feet, and he would throw a rocket back to me, head-high. Kids shouldn't have arm problems as long as they're on a routine and doing some of that long tossing. Cade never had a sore arm until he was in the pros.

I taught him to pitch inside. "I don't want you to hit anybody, but throw inside and make them come to you." I also told him if somebody charged him, just stay on top of the mound and keep your glove on. Make them come up to you, although that never happened. He was like Roger Clemens. Maybe not as nasty as Clemens, but he wasn't afraid to come inside to a guy. I'm against throwing at people's heads, and hopefully the pitchers are as well. Pitchers now drive me crazy. I was watching a game where a pitcher gave up three home runs and he never came inside to these hitters. The batters are going into the ball, not afraid of being hit. When I played, if the guy in front of me hit a home run I was very leery of getting into the box. That's how we looked at things.

There was one Little League all-star game Cade was pitching. There's always a big kid on the other team, a big, strong kid who hits home runs. And the other team had a kid who hit a couple of home runs the day before. I said, "Cade, just throw everything inside to him. Bust him inside." I moved my outfielders way in, because I knew if he hit it, it would be a home run anyway, so what's the sense of playing deep on a Little League field? First two times up, Cade struck him out. And Cade was 12, facing a kid who was nearly a foot taller than him.

The third time up, it got to two strikes and I had my catcher move a foot inside. Cade threw a ball right down the middle. The catcher was so far over that he couldn't reach it. The ball hit the umpire right in the mask. But the umpire had the guts to call strike three.

I didn't let him throw curveballs as he grew up. Mainly it was just fastballs, and once in a while he would throw a curveball although that was very seldom. He had a great curveball. That ball could really drop. He actually picked up the circle change from watching Nolan Ryan on television and seeing how Ryan gripped the ball.

Travel teams were around although not to the extent that they are now. They always wanted these kids to be in these high-profile tournaments that all these colleges would see. Nah, I don't go that route. I thought Cade was good enough to make it on his own without help from these guys. He's got me. He just worked with me. Why am I going to let him go work with some guy unless I thought the guy was one of my buddies who knew something about baseball? I know just as much as any of them about how to get ready, how to hit, how to throw, etc. A lot of guys approached me about Cade but I told them to take a hike. We didn't need it.

Even if I had a teenage son now, I wouldn't have him play in a travel league. I don't really believe in it. If the kid has talent and plays normal baseball throughout the year, I think that's good enough. Some of these kids wind up playing too much. If there is somewhere close to home where they can play almost all year, then fine. But I'm not going to ship them off to New Jersey, Nebraska or Kansas just to play in some stupid tournament. There are parents in my area, and I guess around the country,who pay all this money to let their kid go to Cooperstown and play in some Hall of Fame game. I don't get that, but that's because I played the game. If the kid has talent, I guarantee you that the teams will find him and he is going to get signed. If these scouts can go to the Dominican Republic or South Korea, or anywhere else in the world where they go to find talent, they're going to be able to find it in this country. There's no doubt. But people waste so much money on this stuff. All the traveling plus the money they spend on equipment and uniforms. It's crazy. These parents want their kids to be Major League players. I don't blame them. Remember much less than 1% ever get there.

A lot of people have moved to South Orange County because they think they have a kid who is a stud player and they think the kid will learn more and become a better athlete, and they'll have a better chance for a college scholarship, if not sign professionally.

Every dad thinks his kid is the next Mickey Mantle or the next Sandy Koufax. It doesn't work that way. Very, very few even sign, let alone get the chance to play pro ball, let alone go to the majors, let alone win the World Series as a rookie. Why did it happen to me? I don't know. But I'm sure glad it did.

I still help out some people on the side. I have an excellent painter, Jesse Ulrich, who wanted me to watch his kid. Like a lot of dads, he's talking about what a good hitter his kid is. You know how that goes. Usually the kid isn't that good. But the kid came over and he could swing the bat. His dad never played the game but he's done a good job with him. There wasn't much advice I could give him, even at 10 years old. I'd throw fastballs inside and he would get around on it. The kid can hit. It will be fun to see what he does in seven years.

Cade's high school coach was Bob Zamora, who I had played against in college. He was an infielder who played two seasons in the minor leagues. Zamora has been the coach at the school since it opened in 1977, and recently won his 600th game. He's had a great career. Bob is a good guy who I liked a lot. He's good with the kids. I would say he's the best coach in the area, if not in the state of California. I'd talk to him like a typical parent would. He'd listen to me, but I was out of the picture. I wasn't going to tell him how to coach Cade.

Then Cade went on to play at Saddleback Junior College. The name of the coach was Jack Hodges. Jack coached at Saddleback for about 20 years. He coached at Laguna Hills High School before that. The assistant coach at Saddleback was Bob Schellenberg, who had been my high school teammate. It's a small world. The players, Cade included, loved Bob.

I think Saddleback usually had more talent than any other junior college in California, but they never could win. Like I tell people, South Orange County has the best athletes in the world. Just pick a sport. But you have to realize only the top people sign. Carson Palmer was from the area and went to USC before playing in the NFL. And another NFL quarterback, Mark Sanchez, went to Mission Viejo High School before playing for USC. He actually has the most playoff wins for any Jet quarterback.

Damion Easley, who was an All-Star and had a nice career, played at Lakewood High School and Long Beach City College. Travis d'Arnaud, the catcher for the Mets in the 2015

World Series, went to Lakewood High School. The Minnesota Twins used the number one pick in the 2017 draft on Royce Lewis, a shortstop who played right down the road from us. Those are exceptions but people see that and get dollar signs in their eyes.

Look at the NBA. There are 12 guys on a team and there are 30 teams. So there are only about 300 players in the league. What are the odds a kid is going to make it all the way to the NBA? A lot slimmer than making it to Major League Baseball, where each team has 25 guys. But there are amateur rankings where these so-called scouts rank the best 10- and 11-year olds. Football is a bit different because there are 53 players on each team, and there are two more pro teams than other leagues. And baseball has more players than basketball, but that doesn't stop these basketball parents from signing kids up for everything in hopes of going pro. But I don't care what sport it is. Even if it's an individual sport like tennis. You have to be the top of the top to sign professionally.

A lot of parents live their lives through their kids and it doesn't work. The kid might rebel, he might get hurt, and he might not like it. It was nice coaching Cade because it was something he wanted to do. If he had lost interest in it, I would have backed off. I wasn't going to push him. Too many parents make that mistake. I wasn't forcing him to play because his old man had played baseball. I had my career. I played 10 years of pro baseball and won a World Series. I was a good teacher because I had the experience and knew what he had to do. And he had the talent to play and was willing to work hard. I worked his butt off. Some of his friends came to work out with him and they couldn't do it. They quit but Cade kept working and stayed with me. I thought the coaches he had might be tougher, but they weren't. I was tougher on Cade than they were. He needed a push, I gave him that push, and he responded.

But again, I had the experience of playing professional baseball. If I had just been a regular parent who hadn't played sports it might have been a different story. I might have fallen for that line of "Yeah, I can get your boy a scholarship" or "Yeah, you can buy these tapes and I'll send them to scouts and he can get a scholarship to a four year school." I had been through that stuff. I didn't care for scouts when I played. I remember one guy telling me that he would give me the opportunity to play. Screw that. What does that mean? You're going to sign me for nothing? So it helped Cade having a dad who played. I also think kids should play all sports if they want. It seems more specialized now. Obviously, there's so much more money to be made playing professionally than there was 50 years ago.

Now kids focus on one sport because they can master one and hope to get the big contract. There are studies that show the children that only play one sport enjoy it less because there is more pressure to make it to the pros. It's good to play a few sports just to break up the monotony. Then when they get older, they can realize what they're specialty is and focus on the one sport that they're best at. But not when you're 12 years old and playing travel ball and winter ball all year round. (Maybe throwing all year long is why a lot of amateur pitchers are blowing out their arms, although I don't think that's the case unless the kid is throwing every single day.) I don't like that. I was 18 when I went all in on baseball. I don't think you know until a kid is around 16 if they have a chance at a scholarship. If the kids want to play basketball as well, let them play basketball. If they want to golf, let them go out and swing the club. Now if that's the only one they want to play, then fine. Baseball was the only sport Cade played because that was the only one he was interested in.

When Cade was a teenager, we would go to the local field three or four times a week to play catch and he'd get further and further away until he was loose. He'd get back over 300 feet and just start throwing rockets to me. I mean, like 10 feet off the ground. He had a great arm. Once you get that arm loose, it feels like there's a heating pad inside your shoulder. And because you're so loose and so warm, that's when you throw as hard as you can. It worked for me and I think it would work for everybody. That's what makes your arm stronger. You can make you arm stronger if you long toss, which I don't think most people do anymore. I see so many outfielders now have terrible arms.

Cade was a shortstop in college, and would only pitch in relief. Houston had a good scout who really liked him named Bob King. He noticed Cade as a shortstop. King saw him throw the ball from the shortstop position to first base and was impressed. Houston picked him in the 15th round of the 1992 draft as a pitcher, even though King hadn't seen him pitch. Cade wanted more money than they offered, but they still had his rights. It was what was known as a draft and follow. Cade had dropped out of school because of everything that happened with David, and his heart wasn't really into baseball. But the Astros came around the next year offering more. I asked Cade what would happen if they offered $250,000. Cade said, "I don't know, Dad." So they come in and offer him $250,000 to sign. He turned it down and took a scholarship to Pepperdine, the school that had won the NCAA title in 1992. Don't let people say that money is not important. Like when somebody says, "It's not the money." Yes, it is the money.

Cade could have returned to Saddleback, because he had one year of eligibility left. Jack Hodges obviously wanted him to stay. I found out through some sources that other schools were interested in Cade, including USC. Hodges never told us because he wanted Cade to remain at Saddleback. But he still ended up at Pepperdine, which worked out well. It might have been better if he ended up at USC, thinking about it after the fact, but it worked out well for Cade. There are no complaints. And what a campus Pepperdine has. It's Malibu overlooking the ocean. Not a bad place to go to school. It's nice being in a warm place like California where you can always stay in shape. That's one of the things that helped me make the majors.

Cade played at Pepperdine for a year. He was the best pitcher on the team and the best pitcher in the league. But he wasn't thrilled there. The coach, Andy Lopez, had told him that he would play and hit. He wouldn't just be pitching. But these college coaches will say anything to get you in. Lopez said, "Yeah, you'll hit and play," but that didn't happen. When Cade first got to Pepperdine, they wouldn't even pitch him. That's crazy. They gave him the best scholarship that you can give a player and they weren't even bothering to use him. But once they started playing him, he took off. Cade would be warming up in the bullpen before a game and all these scouts would be watching him throw.

The Mets had the number one pick overall in the 1994 draft and Paul Wilson from Florida State University was the big stud in college at the time. I was talking to somebody with the Mets and said, "Why don't you take my boy number one? We'll take less money just for the honor of being taken number one." But they didn't go for that and they took Wilson. The thing I remember from Wilson's career was that he was hitting once and Kyle Farnsworth threw at him. Wilson charged the mound and Farnsworth just annihilated him.

The Angels were talking about drafting Cade with the sixth overall pick. They came to the house the night before the draft and said they wanted him. They offered $700,000 as a pre-draft offer. I don't even know if they can do that anymore. I said, "Hey, he wants to sign with you guys but I can't accept it because there are no guarantees that he'll still be there." One of the Angels' representatives was Bob Harrison, who had grown up with my dad. When I was born, Bob was in the hospital with my parents. And I had coached Bob's grandson in Little League.

The next day, we didn't get a call from the Angels. I was really upset because they passed on him. They ended up taking McKay Christiansen, an outfielder who went to high school in Fresno. And they gave him his $700,000. Now that shows how stupid the Angels were. The guy they picked number one was a Mormon who was off to do missionary work for two years and he ended up never playing for the Angels.

If I had to do it over again, or at least if things were like they are now, I'd have asked Scott Boras to represent Cade. Now the agents run the game. Not that I'm a fan of the agents and players telling the front office how things are going to be, but I'd use the system to our advantage.

Detroit selected Cade with the 18th overall pick in the 1994 draft and he got a $825,000 bonus, plus college tuition, room and board if he went back to school. It was much more than what the Angels had offered.

Funny thing is, the Mets didn't pick Cade like I would've liked them to, but I went to Shea Stadium a few months after the draft for a Old-Timers' Game. They did a 25th anniversary tribute to the Miracle Mets, and they had guys from the 1969 team play a group of players from all the other teams in the majors. None of the Mets were wearing 1969 jerseys. We all had custom jerseys from that era. I was wearing the Mets style jersey from the 80s, with the racing stripe down the sides.

The major league legends had Curt Flood, Rick Wise and Felix Millan to name a few. Juan Marichal pitched for them. Some Cubs like Glenn Beckert, Don Kessinger and Randy Hundley played. Randy's son, Todd, was on the Mets at the time. Paul Blair and Merv Rettenmund represented the Orioles, and Earl Weaver was coaching first base. And we had most of our lineup. I drove in Wayne Garrett with a double to left off Ron Reed. Wayne scored from first and was one of the fastest guys running that day. I had a nice, easy swing the opposite way. You don't have to swing hard. All you have to do is get the bat out in front, get it on the good part of the bat and let the bat do the work.

I had the only RBI as we won 1-0. That was the last year the Mets did an Old-Timers' day. So, to date, I'm the last player with an RBI in a Mets Old-Timers' game.

Cade didn't make it to the majors. A few years after being drafted, Cade hurt his arm and was out of the game. I don't think he really enjoyed it. I don't think he liked the professional game. Cade was the opposite of me. I loved the game; I loved the lifestyle.

I knew Glenn Ezell from when I played in the minors. We had been teammates at Williamsport and Memphis where he was one of the catchers. Glenn stayed in the game as a coach and front-office man and was with the Tigers for many years. I saw him one time and Glenn said, "You know, your boy doesn't seem like he's having fun out there." If you don't like what you're doing, how can you be successful at it? You've got to really enjoy what you're doing to be successful.

Cade preferred playing in the field and batting to pitching anyway. But the Tigers drafted him as a pitcher. He pitched for two years in the Tigers organization, and was traded to the San Diego organization like his dad was.

He hurt his arm because he was lifting weights in the offseason. That's what happened with my son. He was 6'3" and only weighed about 175 pounds. It was a great athletic frame. Guys want to get bigger and stronger, but it doesn't work that way in baseball, especially for a starting pitcher. You want those muscles to be long and lean. You don't want bulky muscles. Detroit started having him lift weights in the offseason, which led to him having a stronger upper body so he had to change his throwing motion and he hurt his arm. That was dumb on my part for allowing him to go back to Detroit in the offseason. I thought they knew something about weightlifting but apparently they didn't. Maybe that's why these guys in the game today have all these injuries. They have too many muscles.

Another good thing that came out of his contract was that Detroit paid for his education at Pepperdine if he went back to school. He went back to school and earned his degree in business.

Taylor was a good athlete. In school she played basketball, softball, soccer and ran track and field. I would go watch her play soccer, which is not my favorite sport to watch. I'd always tell parents soccer is a great conditioner for other sports. Those people would get so mad at me for saying that. I just don't care for soccer. But it is a great conditioner because of all the running they have to do. I helped coach a soccer team for one year. I didn't know the positions, didn't know the rules, nothing. I told them to kick the ball first. Be aggressive and get to the ball first. And they did. I never really cared for the game, the way guys would fall to the ground without being hit. I don't think it will really catch on in this country the way they want it to. How can it? It is a communist sport.

When I coached baseball, you could say things to the umpire, and get on him a little bit. Soccer is a different game. You couldn't say too much to a referee. They are out there with their shorts on and these high socks that go up to their knees. One time I was getting on a referee and making comments, and he threw me out of the soccer game. When that happened, I told myself that this sport wasn't for me. I never coached it again.

When Taylor played soccer she was very aggressive. She was a real good player, possible scholarship material although she didn't pursue it after high school. I told her I would be at her games because I knew how aggressive she would be on the field. So one day I skip a game which was out of our area and I went to work out at LA Fitness. I guess you know where this is going. Taylor calls me and tells me that there was a fight during the game. My little gal had been taken down by a slide from this older woman. They started mouthing off and Taylor punched her in the face. That's why I always tried to go to her games. She'd get into scraps once in a while. At least she had the gumption to call me. She didn't tell her mother at first but at least she told me. That was the last episode she had on the soccer field.

She used to date a guy who was a centerfielder on a team that won the College World Series. He was a good centerfielder and had a really strong arm. He always used to dive for balls in the outfield. I told him, "When I was playing, those balls that you dove for, I would be waiting for them." That used to drive him crazy, this older guy bragging about his defense. He also didn't like that I called him a dumbass for diving headfirst into bases. He would dive headfirst into home, headfirst into first, anywhere. He ended up needing a few back surgeries.

Our son, Corte, has three beautiful boys with his wife, Michelle. Corte is really involved in Little League coaching. Two of the kids play baseball, and the other one is into water polo. He enjoys watching his boys play sports. He is also our quiet child. He doesn't talk too much. In fact, after David passed away, I could hardly get Corte to talk at all. He and David were only three years apart and they were very, very close. I would try to talk to Corte about David but he wouldn't say anything. It's been like that for years until recently when he started talking about his younger brother. They did everything together and they loved each other very much. As I said before about David being a good athlete, Corte was a good athlete also. He was the top pitcher in our Little League at age 12 and he played baseball through high school and was one of the top players at Mission Viejo High School. He hurt his arm and didn't get a chance to play in college because of the injury. I think he could've played professionally had he not hurt his arm, but GOD has blessed him with a beautiful family and he is a genius at his work which is in the technology field, which I know nothing about. I don't understand what he really does but I think he designs some kind of programs for Irvine Water District, and does very well for himself financially. He and his brother, Cade, are just the opposite of their dad when it comes to working with tools. They have helped me so much with woodwork and different jobs around the house that I can't do, or won't do.

Heather has four kids with her husband, Max. Heather is very talented and I think she could have played sports but she had no interest in them. I know I say this about all our children but I believe that she might have been the best athlete of the bunch. You should see her throw a baseball. She was our first child and grew up a lot in the baseball life in terms of doing a lot of traveling. She was a good baby. We'd go out to restaurants and she never cried. She is a great mother and wife. She and her husband have done well over the years. Heather is excellent with money and budgeting, and follows Scripture on how to use money wisely. She and Taylor are very good savers. When she and Cade were younger, I used to give them 25 cents for each Scripture that they would memorize. Their dad was a big spender. She has continued to study the word of God ever since. I suggested to her that she could help a lot of people by teaching them how to use money wisely.

Cade is a fireman and enjoys what he does. Taylor lives in Austin, Texas. She married Ty Estes a few years ago and they're doing well. She covers the Texas Longhorns football team. I usually don't bring up football because she can talk about it forever. Right now Sheridan and I have 10 grandchildren and there could be more down the line.

The main blessing for our kids is that they are followers of JESUS CHRIST. There are a lot of families, especially in California where the kids are staying at home for longer periods of time. To buy a house, or even rent, in California can be pretty expensive. I'm glad that our children are on their own, contributing to society. I guarantee you that they wouldn't want to live with me anyway, so they busted their butts and got out. And they have all done well. They're making decent money and they're happy with their lives. There are no complaints at all there.

It is funny how the kids know my background and that I was on the 1969 Mets, but we don't talk about it a lot. When Sheridan and I were in New York in 2009 for the 40th anniversary celebration, Taylor came with us, although the other kids didn't. Taylor likes this stuff the most because of her interest in sports. She has scrapbooks and enjoys memorabilia. The other kids aren't as interested.

I don't like talking about my kids unless other people bring it up. For example, Sheridan and I were having dinner with this nice couple, and the woman was always talking about her children. We just let them talk. I love my kids, and I love my grandkids, but I don't bring them up. I found over the years the minute that somebody asks you about your kids, if you open up and start talking about them, they will interrupt you and start talking about their own kids. I zip my lips, smile and let them talk.

To this day, a lot of people probably still don't know that we've lost a child. Even people I've known for years. If somebody asks how many kids I have, I say "five," not "four but one is dead."

I don't know if people are really that interested in my family or if they just want to make conversation. Most people see someone and say, "Hi, how are you?" That's followed by the person saying that they're good, and "How are you?" And so on. Well, with me, if someone asks how I'm doing, I say, "Doing well, thank you." And I leave it at that. Because I don't know if people are really that concerned. Very seldom do I ask how they're doing. I appreciate them asking, though. I really do.

According to Tommy Lasorda, "Talking about your troubles is no good. Eighty percent of your friends don't care and the rest are glad."

My dad died on June 8, 1997, thirty years to the day after I signed with the Mets. He was the best man I ever met. My mother died seven years later. I think about them a lot.

186

And I think about Sheridan's parents a lot, and how much fun we all used to have on Christmas. Death stinks for those left behind. But that's part of living on this earth. You're going to die sometime. That's part of the deal. You never know what's going to happen. We think we're in control, but we're not.

Lloyd Jr. is in the Sonora High School Hall of Fame, where he was a teacher and principal for many years. He got a job at the school over 120 other applicants and he still lives there with his wife. He has a Master's degree and wrote his thesis on the effects of Astroturf on sports. He's retired and lives in Sonora.

My brother, Jack, passed away in the early '90s, and we're still not exactly sure what happened. He had some alcohol issues. He graduated from high school in 1969, and was in the movement at that time. I think our society changed when Kennedy was shot, and after that The Beatles came to the country, and I think they changed it big time, and then the Vietnam War. It was the complete opposite of how it was in the '50s.

Jack had been in the service for a few years. His lifestyle wasn't the best, but he was a good guy. Jack was hitching a ride home one night, a trucker picked him up, and when Jack got out he dropped down to get something in a bag. He fell and the truck rolled over him and crushed him. He was a good kid but had some issues, like we all have issues.

Cade was married in Hawaii in 2004. I'm in a golf shop a few days before the wedding and all of a sudden I hear some guy say, "Rocket Rod Gaspar." It was some local guy who had seen my name on a register or recognized me in the clubhouse. I hadn't been in Hawaii in nearly 30 years. That nickname always stuck with me. The majority of my handball buddies call me "The Rocket." They don't call me Rod. It was nice that the guy remembered me. Those fans in Hawaii like their sports.

After I left the game, I was trying to stay in shape but I was putting on a little weight. I was under 180 pounds when I retired, and wanted to stay under 190. You have to lay off the mashed potatoes and gravy. Some guys can be heavier with success. Mickey Lolich was a great pitcher for the Tigers and once joked, "All the fat guys watching me say to their wife, 'See, there's a fat guy doing OK. Bring me another beer.'"

But I started playing racquetball at a recreational center. I got pretty good and played in a local tournament. I was in my late 40s and they asked me if I wanted to be in the B division. I told them no, put me in the open division, which was the top division. The guy warned me that there were tough players in it, but I said it was alright. I went through my bracket and beat the top seed to get to the final match.

I'm going against this young Mexican guy who didn't look like he was in the best of shape. He was a little chunky. He was about half my age and could really hit that ball low. He had me diving all over the place, and I'm not a diver. Even when I played baseball I rarely drove because I seldom had to. I played well but he beat me.

Cade was there and he saw his dad get beat. He came out of the stands when it was over and he had tears in his eyes. I said, "Son, remember one thing. You're not going to win all the time, but I guarantee you, you'll win most of the time. As long as you win most of the time, you're going to be successful in life."

They usually crack up at my sayings. But it's true. If you're successful most of the time, you'll be successful in life. I sure wasn't successful against that kid on the racquetball court. I pretty much stopped with the sport after that and focused on handball. And I'm glad I did.

I won my first handball national title in 1996, at age 50. I kept racking up the titles. Tournaments would be over four days so there would be at least four matches. Sometimes, there might be five or six matches if it was a bigger draw. It can wear it out. I went to Chicago, Memphis, Las Vegas, Houston, winning all over the country. I didn't know how many I had until some guy told me I had eight national titles. Eight? OK. So I told myself that I guess I had to win two more. I went with a friend to Oregon. My friend needed one more to get to 10 and I joked, "Yeah, I'll win it for you." So we won the doubles title which gave him his 10th. In 2012, I won a doubles tournament with Dan Scilley, a guy from Montana, which was my 10th. I haven't played any national tournaments since then. I think I could still keep winning at my age if I wanted to continue playing competitively but I have no desire to do it at this time. Maybe my desire to play again will change in the future. Don't get me wrong, although I'm not in national tournaments, I still play handball recreationally and for the workout.

Yours truly can still hit the ball hard and play well. It's just like anything else. You have to want to play it. You have to have that desire to go out and compete and win. You'd be surprised by how many handball players there are in this country because it's not a publicized sport, but they have a national sport. Jake Plummer, the former quarterback, and his family are big in it. His brother runs a place in Idaho. It's a national game but it's not a good spectator sport. If you watch in person, it's still kind of tough to follow. And can you imagine trying to film it? Handball players would watch it and like it. I don't watch it because I don't care to watch it. I really don't watch any sports other than baseball, and I watch very little of that.

There are 85-year-old guys who still play handball. When I go to LA Fitness, there are still about 16 guys who play. There was a buddy of mine who was 75 and he had a hip replaced just so he could keep playing handball. I think that's a little sick. These guys are just fanatics for the game. A lot of older guys beat younger guys. They're not expecting us to be diving on the floor and scraping our knees. In New York, they have one-wall, three-wall, and four-wall, which are indoor courts. I always played indoors. I've played at the New York Athletic Club, which overlooks Central Park. And I played at the Downtown Athletic Club, which is where they used to present the Heisman Trophy. Those courts are the nicest I ever played on. Real good floors, the ball would jump off that court.

As I said earlier, I've won 10 national handball tournaments, which they call a grandmaster. They gave me a sweater for it. The United States Handball Association wanted to present me with it. They wanted me to get on a stage and they would present me with it in front of everybody. I told them that I wasn't interested. If they wanted to give me the sweater next time I saw them, fine. But I didn't go to the dinner and banquet where they honored two other guys. One of the guys being honored called me and asked me to go to the banquet. Sometimes I feel uncomfortable with that stuff. If it's the Mets honoring the 1969 players, all of us as a team, then I'm fine with that.

As I am getting older, it's tough to push past anything because my heart may go out of whack because I have atrial fibrillation. I love competing on the handball court, especially if the games are close. To me it's like hitting in the bottom of the ninth with the winning run on second base. The pressure is fun. I have been playing handball since the early 1980s. At my age I'm a little banged up but competition in sport is so much fun. I've always loved it and hopefully I can play longer.

It's the mental aspect of the game. That was my attitude when I was younger and even later on when I was playing handball. If you think you're tired, Rod, you're tired. I can get fired up when I have to. Fire in the belly.

A few years ago, I couldn't even lift my arms and I had to give up playing handball for a year. I went to all these doctors to see what the heck was wrong with my shoulders. I went to a nerve doctor, a neurosurgeon, a neurologist, I went to a doctor who stuck needles in me, I went to my orthopedic guy, and I had an MRI done. Eventually, he told me that he thought I had frozen shoulders. There was no injury either. I woke up one morning and couldn't lift my arms. The doctors could never figure out why it happened. My wife had a frozen shoulder years before, and she couldn't lift one of her arms. I started exercising in a pool to loosen the shoulders up. The guy said it would take about one year before they loosen up, and that's exactly what happened. Twelve months later, I got the use of my arms back again. And now I'm back to playing handball, even if I don't have the fire to compete in tournaments anymore. But during that year the pain was so severe to a point where I couldn't even get to sleep. I would get no sleep. I don't wish that pain on anybody, except maybe a few politicians. It couldn't be near the pain David went through when he had leukemia. The orthopedic doctor was saying it was strange to have the problem in both arms at the same time...a frozen shoulder in one arm, OK, but two at the same time? I've had some unique things happen to me. That's Rod Gaspar for you. I get to win a World Series in my first year, which doesn't happen to too many guys, and I get frozen shoulders in both arms.

In scripture, Philippians 4:6, says, "Be anxious for nothing." If you think about it, that applies to everything we do: talking, driving a car, eating, standing in line. We're all anxious and we're all in a hurry. If we worked on taking more time, usually it helps you get things done quicker than actually trying to finish it real fast. I would tell my kids that before a Little League game. You need relaxed concentration but stay pumped, which is kind of a paradox. But it's good for hitting. Relax, relax, relax and then explode. Grip the bat firmly but not like you want to strangle it. It makes you too tense anyway. It applies to baseball, it applies to talking, anything. If you back off and relax a little bit, there would be a lot less stress.

Baseball Today

Professional sport owners shouldn't interfere, but now they do. But with a team like the New England Patriots, the owner is smart enough to let Bill Belichick run things. In baseball, they used to let the manager make the decisions, at least when I played. Gil Hodges certainly made his own decisions. Now the owners and all these other guys who know nothing about baseball make these decisions and don't let the manager do what he does best. The game is basically now run by non-baseball people, which I find ridiculous. It would be like me running a business I know nothing about. If you're going to win, you need baseball people in there that know the game like we did.

We had Gil Hodges, a former All-Star, as our manager. Johnny Murphy, another former All-Star, was our general manager. They ran the club and they did a good job. It's a whole new game now but I think it'd be a lot better for the teams, in most cases, if they had baseball people running the organization. The owner can be whoever he or she wants to be, but hire good baseball people. It's nice to see Derek Jeter become a part-owner of the Marlins as opposed to Jeffrey Loria, who only cared about the bottom line. Loria owned the Expos, and then Bud Selig, the owner of the Milwaukee Brewers and so-called "Commissioner of Baseball," just gave him the Marlins. And remember the Marlins used to be run by Wayne Huizenga, the Blockbuster Video guy. He won the 1997 World Series and then got rid of all the players and sold the team, and baseball allowed it to happen. That is criminal. That was under Selig's watch also. I'm not a big fan of a lot of the owners and how they run this great game. I think some of the owners do care, but why they allow some of these owners to stay in the game, I have no idea. A "commissioner," like Selig, who was also an owner is just going to help the other owners who are in it for themselves. When these guys use the expression "for the good of the game," that is so much B.S. It should be "for the good of the owner's."

While fans call owners cheap, there are some owners that need to be protected from themselves. The Angels got burned giving Josh Hamilton a five-year, $125 million deal. And now they give Justin Upton a five-year, $106 million deal. Doesn't Artie Moreno, the Angels owner, get it? I guess he hasn't learned his lesson. Plus, Moreno has not had a decent front office guy since general manager Bill Stoneman, that's right, a former Major League Baseball player, who guided the Angels to their only World Series championship in 2002. Maybe Upton will turn out to be worth it (but I don't think so). Very few guys are worth that level of money. Why not take that money and get a few guys who could fill different needs around the diamond?

Giancarlo Stanton is making over a quarter of a billion dollars. That's crazy, even if he is an MVP winner who hit 59 homers in his last season with the Marlins. These guys might not be able to play down the road. Even Albert Pujols, one of my favorite players, was signed for insane money. I love Albert, but once he's not putting up the numbers with the Angels that he did with the Cardinals, now they're stuck with him in a sense because of the long contract.

In the early '90s, when these contracts were really starting to take off, someone asked Joe DiMaggio how he would negotiate with George Steinbrenner. And Joe said, "George, you and I are about to become partners." That sounds about right. He was the first $100,000 player in the late 40s. Imagine what he would get now. And the most money my favorite player, Mickey Mantle, ever made in a season was $100,000. Those guys were still set after their careers with other work and autograph signings.

In my rookie season, I hit .228 and played really good defense, with 12 outfield assists and six double plays started. Now that would probably get me a few million dollars per year. Isn't that nice? Now the minimum salary is over half a million dollars, at $507,500. Imagine that. I made $10,000 in 1969 and I was living good. They hold down the salaries for the rookie contracts and then after a few years, they make the big money. If you have a few decent seasons, you can be looking at tens of millions of dollars. It's unbelievable.

Whitey Herzog mentioned that all the Mets had to do was draw one million people to Shea Stadium, and that would pay all the expenses for the whole year. It would pay the major league salaries, minor league salaries, and all that other stuff. Anything over a million in attendance was pure profit for the team. Of course that's nothing now, especially with all the television contracts teams have in addition to the paying fans at the games. The Mets drew over four million fans during the last season at Shea Stadium. And there are all the property rights teams have with selling replica jerseys. What a racket that is. That's a fairly new thing for the fans. If you watch the games from 1969, no fans had jerseys on. A few had caps or jackets. During the World Series, a lot of spectators had coats and ties on. They were all decked out to go watch a baseball game. Not like nowadays. It's a whole new world.

And the players get bonus money at the end of the year called licensing fees. We never received anything. I got a set of golf clubs when I signed a bat contract with Louisville Slugger.

That was about it. Marvin Miller was the guy who started it all and I wouldn't be surprised if a lot of players today didn't know who he is.

It's not just team sports. Even the top golfers make a lot of money. Those golfers should all get on their knees and thank Arnold Palmer because he's the guy who started it, just like baseball players should get on their knees and thank Marvin Miller (also, along with Gil, why isn't Marvin in the baseball Hall of Fame?). Palmer started the golf craze in this country because he was winning when TV started televising the sport. Arnold was the guy who started the golf station on TV as well.

It's amazing to see when a team deals with an incoming player from Japan. Before the Red Sox signed Daisuke Matsuzaka, they had to pay $51 million just to negotiate with him! Then $52 million more to actually sign him to a contract. The Angels recently signed Shohei Ohtani. So teams had to pay a fee to negotiate, and I read that they want a letter from each major league team that's interested in signing him. They want to know every little thing about the team. And the Angels signed Ohtani for money that wasn't that bad but now once they signed him, it turns out he might be injured. That a boy, Artie. What's a few more million down the drain? Seriously, I hope the kid can play.

Living in California, I can't believe the Dodgers have a TV deal that actually blocks a lot of people in Los Angeles from seeing Dodgers home games. I don't know why they can't get that done, and reward the loyalty that the fans have shown them over the years. And it shows how much the fans care, that they keep going to the games when it looks like the team doesn't care about the fans. Remember what I said earlier, the owners are in the game for "the good of the owners." How many billions, not millions, but billions of dollars to these owners need? What a racket.

I wonder about my old team, the Padres. Why are they always so bad? They were good with Steve Garvey and a young Tony Gwynn when they won the pennant in 1984. And then they went back to the World Series in 1998 when Gwynn was a veteran. But for most of the time, they're not good. They were one of the worst teams when I played with them.

George Steinbrenner is a guy I would have loved to play for even though I never met him. What I like is that he took care of a lot of his former players. George would pay his former players to go around the suites in the stadium and talk to the high rollers. Even when he fired his managers, he would keep them on as scouts or some other position in the organization. And he tried to take care of down-and-out guys like Darryl Strawberry and Dwight Gooden. Steinbrenner had a heart for his players even if he had a funny way of showing it at times. And of course there were the back-and-forth battles he had with Billy Martin. Billy had his issues, like we all do, but he was a great manager. Not like some of the guys in the dugout now.

The game changed under Selig. The owners pick one of their own to run the game. Is that a monopoly or what? I guess he lasted so long because all the owners were making money. The other part is that there's only one main commissioner as opposed to league presidents that they did away with. There's not as much rivalry between the leagues. It used to be just the All-Star Game and the World Series. Now there's season-long interleague play. And the umpires aren't separated by league anymore.

I have a few baseballs, and the older ones say "National League Baseball" on it, and the new ones say "Major League Baseball" on it. I was watching some 1969 World Series games, and during Game Four, there's a little delay as one of the umpires is talking to Seaver when he's on the mound. The next day, the announcers mention that it was due to the fact that someone noticed Seaver was using an American League ball. I don't know if the baseballs were different other than the fact that they had different stamps on them.

Before the 2017 season, Noah Syndergaard put on a lot of muscle and he already threw 97, 98 miles per hour. He was already an All-Star pitcher who could dominate teams. How fast do you have to throw? It's like what happened with our son when he bulked up and hurt his throwing motion, and then he hurt his arm. That was the end of his 90-something-mile per hour fastball.

There is a place for it but I don't think a lot of pitchers should do it for their upper bodies and shoulders. Nolan Ryan started his own routine after he found some barbells and dumbbells under the stadium when he was an Angel. I read his book about conditioning program and training. Oh my goodness, what an animal. He developed his own program and obviously it worked for him. But he was different and had a perfect body for his great mechanics because he knew what exercises to do to keep him strong. That's why he pitched until he was 46.

But he wasn't doing that stuff when he was on the Mets. None of us were. The difference with Nolan's lifting was that he was doing lower body workouts and not trying to bulk up his arm. Seaver was another lower body guy. That's where you get the power from. It's less stress on the shoulder. Gentry was all arm basically. Hodges and Rube Walker talked about that and they didn't think he'd last. They didn't think he'd get a lot of years in the big leagues because he was all arm. And they were right. He only lasted a couple of years with the Mets and then Atlanta.

I still love the game but I'm not fired up about the people who run it. I might be nitpicking but I think a lot of guys I played with feel the same way. These are just my views of the game as a former player who is not involved with any team. Frank Robinson would probably say again, "Who the hell is Rod Gaspar" to say these things. Some of my former teammates who are still in baseball might disagree, but I don't think so. How about when a coach goes out to the mound and the pitcher covers his face with his glove? What's that about? What are they possibly going to say? And the guys who are talking to them aren't covering their mouths. I don't get it.

There are so many different wind-ups and pitching motions. There's one Angel who moves his foot three times before he throws a pitch, which used to be a balk but they say because it's his regular motion that it's ok. I don't get why starting pitchers pitch out of the stretch. These pitchers take so much time to deliver a baseball. As an outfielder, it destroys your concentration on defense and it destroys the flow of the game. I don't know what pitching coaches and managers do about it. The pitchers might be trying to think too much (baseball players think?). And it becomes a timing issue, especially for the players behind them. The guys want the games rolling. Our five games in the 1969 World Series lasted a combined 11 hours and 43 minutes. I would like someone to compare the pace of those games, even without the commercials being longer now. Try to see what the holdup is, and what wasn't the holdup with us? The pitchers had an idea, and the catchers had an idea. Now, they either don't have an idea, or they have too many and take time to pick one. When pitchers were slow, I would yell, "Throw the f------ ball" from the outfield. Unless they just love being at the ballpark, I don't think people want to be in the stands for four hours watching a baseball game. That's the most boring thing in sports. I felt the same way when I played. Fans want action.

Pitching limits: A guy throws 100 pitches and everybody thinks he's done a great job. When Nolan Ryan took over the Texas Rangers, he got rid of that. He wanted his starters going seven or eight innings. And they won back-to-back pennants. At the 40th anniversary of the 1969 World Series, guys were asking Nolan what's the most pitches he ever threw in a game. Guys are guessing this number, that number. Nolan said he once threw 240 pitches in one game. And he never really had a sore arm or sore shoulder.

He's a great baseball guy. There was a bit of a power struggle in Texas with general manager Jon Daniels, although Nolan had too much class to let it get to that. Nolan left the organization and the Rangers haven't been back to the World Series since. Nolan's son, Reid, ended up becoming the president of the Houston Astros. (Our daughter, Taylor, knew Reid from her reporter days.) And Nolan becomes an advisor for Reid and the Astros, and they win the World Series. He's a real class guy, never badmouthing Daniels, and just doing his thing in Houston. As a side note, occasionally a major league team plays a college team in a spring training game. It's a tune-up for the pros, and a great experience for the kids. In the early '90s, the Rangers played the Texas Longhorns, and Nolan and Reid were the starting pitchers. And Nolan's wife, Ruth, threw out the first pitch.

One of my favorites is outfielders taking three, four or five steps to get rid of the baseball when they're trying to throw someone out. Even in my early 70s, I guarantee you I could get rid of the ball quicker than just about all of these guys. It would take me less than a step and a half. I can't throw the ball like I used to but I could get rid of it fast. Do you believe that? I can. There's no doubt. There are also guys who make a catch and then slide, almost for style.

Everybody catches the ball with one hand now, even the All-Stars. Sooner or later, these guys are going to drop a ball in a clutch situation because you have a tendency to take your eye off the ball. But if you use both hands, you're concentrating on catching the ball. I think it's a hot dog-type thing. Guys want to look cool. Someone actually asked me about that when I was in New York for a reunion in 2009, because it was shortly after the Mets lost a game to the Yankees when Luis Castillo dropped a pop fly at second base and two runs scored. Of course he was stumbling and didn't use two hands. I was on this show taped outside of B.K. Sweeney's Sports Bar and Restaurant in Bethpage, owned by my buddy John Coumatos. And they asked about the Castillo drop, which instantly went down in Mets infamy. I pointed out that so many guys do it, and it was a matter of time until it cost a team like that. It's funny because I was watching a game after that season, and for the final out, the Mets centerfielder made a casual one-hand catch. Why risk dropping it, especially after the Castillo play?

Another pet peeve is guys sliding headfirst into a base. I don't know if Pete Rose started that but when I played guys didn't do that as much. It looks better than sliding feet-first, sure. But there are too many injuries that come out of it. My youngest daughter used to date a player on Cal-State Fullerton team who won the College World Series in 2004. He was a good outfielder and signed a pro contract. I asked him, "Why do you slide head first into the bag?" He continued doing it, of course, and ended up needing some back surgeries. Even Mike Trout was injured diving into a base. I love watching the guy. He's great but that was so stupid. And in the minors the Angels teach the young players not to dive head first into a base. Maybe these guys do it because they started sliding like that at a young age and were used to it.

Another issue I have is with guys not running hard to first on a ground ball. It seems like no big deal but it is a big deal. To me, you want to be aggressive at all times.

The armor these guys wear is amazing now. Elbow pads, wrist guards, foot protection, shin guards. I turned on a game as a guy was down on the ground and I thought he must have really gotten drilled. This batter was face down on the ground. Then they showed the replay. He fouled a ball off his foot. Despite having a guard on his foot, he went down like somebody shot him. I saw that and I started laughing.

Also, doesn't the word "uniform" mean that players are actually supposed to be dressed the same? I thought they were supposed to be standard. When I played, we all generally looked the same. Now guys have compression sleeves, and a lot of other things. Nine guys in a lineup are dressed in nine different ways. And during the playoffs, Joe Maddon wears a beanie. I can't imagine any of the managers when I played doing that. Have a little class.

Pitchers don't throw inside as much. Maybe it's because they feel they can't get in the hitters' heads because the hitters are protected by the umpires. In today's game, if a pitcher throws inside and hits the batter there is a good chance the umpire will throw the pitcher out of the game. I always taught our son to throw inside.

The hitters aren't as aggressive, although they lean out over the plate more because they know they're not in danger of getting hit. Now most hit by pitches are from batters leaning over the plate, not pitchers throwing inside. Most guys go up trying to hit fastballs. If you're a professional baseball player, you can hit a fastball. If I'm up with a man on third with fewer than two outs, I'm looking for a fastball in my zone where I'm going to swing the bat. If it's not there, I'm taking. I see so many of these guys in clutch situations swing at a breaking ball in the dirt on the first pitch. These guys don't think. They flat out don't think. It is not that hard to figure out. Most guys have trouble hitting breaking balls. Be patient, wait for the fastball and adjust. There is more pressure on the pitcher to throw a strike than there is on the hitter.

Here's a little quiz I'd give kids I was coaching, or anybody who was interested. Whose advantage is it in each count? No balls and no strikes: Hitter. One ball and no strikes or any count where the hitter is ahead: Hitter. That one is obvious. Now, how about no balls and one strike? Most people would say the pitcher, but I thought as a hitter it was still to my advantage. Because I felt as long as there weren't two strikes, I didn't have to swing. I'm still looking fastball. Most counts I felt were hitters' counts. The top hitters can look for a fastball and adjust to a curveball. A count of 2-2 might be a push. The pitcher doesn't want to go to 3-2 but he can waste a pitch and the hitter can't. It's hard to throw strikes. If the hitter doesn't panic and isn't afraid of striking out, he can become a good hitter. The best hitters learn to hit with two strikes.

In my 10 years of playing professional baseball, I seldom struck out. I usually made contact when I swung the bat. Judging from some of the Angels games I've been watching, I could've been a superstar with my 1969 batting average of .228. To me, anything under .270 isn't good. Four or five guys in the starting lineup in the game I watched the other day were hitting around the Mendoza line. I wouldn't have stayed with the 1969 Mets all season had I been hitting under .200.

Some of these players have astronomical strikeout numbers but they have some pop, which lets them hang around. A few years ago, Chris Carter hit 41 homers with a .190 batting average for the Brewers. It's funny that he bounces around from team to team, because why get rid of a guy like that if that's what teams are looking for now?

How has the game gotten to the point where they don't care about batting average and only about home runs? I was reading that through the 2017 season, there have been 10 times that a player hit 30 home runs and fewer than 100 hits in a season. Joey Gallo of the Rangers hit 41 home runs and had 94 hits. I was laughing while reading that. That's crazy. Gallo also struck out 196 times.

It used to be a sense of pride not to go down on strikes. In 2017, the league home run leaders were Miami's Giancarlo Stanton (59) and Aaron Judge (52). Then the Yankees went and got Stanton. The funny thing is they combined for more strikeouts in 2017 than Joe DiMaggio had in his entire career.

Some of these guys say it's better to hit the ball in the air, which is one of the dumbest things I've ever heard in my baseball life. Here's another quiz: If you hit the ball in the air, what are the three things that can happen? Home run, pop out or ball dropped for error. And it's a slim chance that a guy is going to hit a home run. So it's one in three chances to get a hit. Ground ball can be a solid hit, a groundout, an error or a soft hit/bad hop single. Three in four chance to get on base. I always tried to hit the ball on the ground.

The way they want guys swinging up is fine for guys hitting home runs but I could see why the guys missing are missing. They're dropping their hands and they miss underneath. If they took that top hand and turned it over they would be better off. If you have a nail and wood, you swing down, you don't turn your wrist up. Coastal Carolina won the College World Series in 2016, and they teach the players to have that uppercut swing. This game started in 1869 and all of a sudden the last few years everybody is teaching players to hit the ball uppercut. It flat doesn't work. Ted Williams had a bit of an uppercut swing but he was Ted Williams. How many Ted Williams's are there? Come on. Some guys are just natural hitters. I thought the way Derek Jeter hit was funky, the way they would pitch him inside and he would have that inside-out swing. But he made it work for him.

I had a good understanding of the strike zone when I played. The National League also had a lot of good umpires. Guys like Tom Gorman and Bill Williams and John Kibler were excellent. Al Barlick was one of the most senior umpires at the time. Augie Donatelli was a nice man and a good home plate umpire. Satch Davidson was good behind the plate and had a big wad of chew in his mouth. Shag Crawford was a nice man who ejected Earl Weaver when he came out to argue balls and strikes during Game Four of the 1969 World Series. There was also Doug Harvey. All you have to know about him was the title for his autobiography was "They Called Me God: The Best Umpire Who Ever Lived." I think everybody respected him. He was very personable. Harry Wendelstedt was good and has family that continued umpiring. Ed Sudol was a guy with a big strike zone. The three longest games in Mets history were a 23-inning loss, a 24-inning loss, and a 25-inning loss, and Sudol was the home plate umpire for all three of those games. There were probably long stretches of time where guys didn't see good pitches to hit.

I didn't really keep tabs on the umpires in terms of little differences they may have had. That was more for the pitchers and catchers to know. I was never too concerned about it. It helped that the umpires were pretty consistent in calling balls and strikes. The leagues were a bit different as the American League had the high strike and the National League had the low strike back then. The strike zone should be from the chest down to the knees. But nowadays it looks like it's from the bottom of the knees to the waist, which is ridiculous. They need to expand it. I noticed while watching some games that the high strike has been called a little more than it used to. I think there was a bigger strike zone when I played.

The veteran players had a little more rope when talking to umpires than a guy like me. Those guys earned the right to discuss situations with the umpire more than a rookie would have. But I knew the strike zone better than most players, even better than a lot of umpires. If I had something to say, it meant I was right. I wasn't just trying to butter a guy up for the next call. One pitch I did have trouble laying off was the high fastball. It looks like it's coming waist high and then all of a sudden, it's up at your shoulders. So I had some trouble laying off that one. I'd swing at it and pop it up. All my years playing, I struggled to let that pitch go by. I think it's tough for a lot of hitters to take that pitch, but I had a great sense of the rest of the strike zone. I usually knew when a ball was a ball, although the umpires sometimes disagreed and they have the final say. I'd try to mix in a few walks, because I did not want to go oh-for-five. It didn't happen very often. But oh-for-five, that's five points off your batting average.

It's tough to say whether the umpires give more leeway to players in today's game, in terms of talking back and forth. They shouldn't. These umpires don't take much, and there are some who won't hesitate to throw a player out of a game.

Umpires are umpires, and they're trained a certain way. You could cuss around them, at least when I played, but the minute you use the word "you," addressing them directly, it's off to the clubhouse. "You S.O.B., you this, you did this," they'll throw you out. So you can cuss, just not directly at them. Actually, you didn't even have to cuss to get thrown out. If you say, "You blew that, you stink, you whatever," they'll throw you out. If I spoke to them, I would call them "ump" or I'd call them by their name if I knew them well enough. I didn't call them "blue" or anything like that. Some guys are able to argue with the umpires and not get thrown out. Tommy Lasorda was really good at that when he was managing the Dodgers.

The outfielders should play in more. There were games at Wrigley Field where the outfielders are so deep. They should play shallow because if it's hit over their head, it's going over the fence. They're not going to catch it when the wind is blowing out, so why play deep? I played shallow when the wind was blowing out there. As a former outfielder watching some games, it's frustrating to see some pop-ups drop in front of the outfielders because they're playing back.

There are other things that shouldn't happen. During the 2017 NLCS, Cubs reliever Carl Edwards Jr. walked pitcher Yu Darvish on four pitches with the bases loaded. Hey man, throw a strike. And then he put his head down. That can't happen. You can't let the other team see that you're down.

The umpires grant so many time outs that it's ridiculous. The hitter requests it, and it seems like the home plate umpire grants it no matter how late. A pitcher can hurt himself stopping in the middle of his motion because some guy called time at the last second. That should not happen. When I was playing, I would give the umpire plenty of time before I called time. And sometimes, you'd step out of the box and the pitch would be delivered for a strike. Not every umpire would call time if we didn't give enough time. That's how it should be. I'm surprised managers don't jump on the umpires more often for allowing it to happen. I don't know how long it's been going on, but it's been a while.

Right now, it's a game favoring the offenses. The 2017 Astros-Dodgers World Series set the record for most home runs in a Fall Classic. The hitters have all the body armor and they're not afraid to lean over the plate even if it's 0-2 or 1-2 in the count. Back in the day, if it was 0-2 or 1-2, we were looking for something inside, which messes up your thinking for hitting an outside pitch, or any kind of pitch. These guys don't have to worry about looking inside because they know if the pitch hits them the pitcher can get thrown out along with the manager. Game 5 of the World Series was 13-12, and nobody was throwing inside. But again, everyone is worried about being ejected or starting a fight or upsetting someone. It has turned into a "I don't want to hurt the 'little darling' game."

Can these pitchers stop walking people? Game 5 of the 2017 World Series was a prime example. Dallas Keuchel walked two batters in the first inning, and they both came around to score. The Dodgers were leading 4-0 in the fourth, and Clayton Kershaw walks George Springer to start the inning, and the Astros tie the game. So now the Astros have tied it, and Colin McHugh comes in from the bullpen and walks the first two batters he faces. And those runs score on a Cody Bellinger homer to make it 7-4. But if that's not enough, Kershaw walks two guys in the bottom of the fifth, so the manager brings in a reliever and they score on a Jose Altuve home run to tie the game at seven.

Houston led 12-9 heading into the ninth inning, and Chris Devenski was pitching because they were afraid to go to Ken Giles, their normal closer. He walked Bellinger to begin the inning. That's inexcusable especially in a World Series. You have a three run lead in the 9th and you walk the leadoff hitter? They should have released the pitcher. Eventually, the Dodgers tied the game. After the game-tying hit, I thought: "Worst Relievers in the History of Baseball...both Teams."

The Astros won 13-12 in 10 innings. Those late innings turn into crapshoots for the managers trying to mix and match because of all those walks. It was a great game for the fans, though.

What is the percentage of batters leading off an inning with a walk come around to score? Not a base hit, but a walk where the pitcher loses the hitter. I don't know the actual number but it feels like it must be at least 70 percent. With all the other statistics baseball's computer wizards have, one would think there would be a stat for this. It is incredible how many times that guy will come around to score. You see it all the time.

"Oh, those bases on balls," as Earl Weaver once said. The pitchers and catchers don't get it. My statistics might be wrong, but I believe the first seven batters in this World Series who reached via the walk all scored. I told my pitchers in Little League, I'd rather see you give up a home run than walk a guy when we have a lead of at least two runs. It is tough to hit a baseball correctly. Here it is, hit it. It doesn't take a genius to figure it out.

There was a funny story I heard from Tony Muser. Outfielder Pat Kelly, a Christian, was playing with the Orioles. Kelly asked manager Earl Weaver, "how is your walk with the LORD, Earl?"

Weaver said, "The only walk I am concerned about is a base on balls."

Another thing is everybody takes such big swings. There are so many shifts, yet nobody tries to bunt for an easy base hit. Few players know how to sacrifice bunt or bunt for a base hit. Brian McCann did try to bunt for a hit. He's slow and was thrown out, but at least he tried. There was another at-bat where McCann struck out on a 3-2 fastball. The question I have is how do you miss a fastball on a 3-2 pitch? What else can you be looking for? You've got to be looking fastball, and once you get it, you have to hit it.

I would bunt for a hit every time up if they put a shift on me, which they wouldn't because I wasn't a pull hitter. But I would do it every single time if I could. The problem is guys get in a certain rut while hitting and it's tough to change. They don't know how to adjust. But they better work on it. I'd be spending all winter trying to perfect that bunt down the third base line. Mickey Mantle was a great bunter whenever he did it. If a powerful man like Mantle, who probably hit the longest home runs ever, can bunt, then we should all be able to bunt. He had amazing speed as well. They say that when he ran, it sounded like a herd of buffaloes coming down the first-base line. Mike Trout might be the closest to that now, with how hard he runs.

To me the top hand chop wood swing works. At least adjust. If Henry Aaron did it, I think it's a pretty good idea to follow.

Ian Kennedy turned his career around once he challenged guys more. He was a young so-so pitcher with the Yankees, trying to figure things out. He went to Arizona and became a 20-game winner. Somebody asked him what changed, and he said that having to bat in the National League showed him how difficult hitting was. So he challenged the hitters. And he's not a big guy, at maybe six feet tall.

There are so many home runs, it's no wonder that guys have ignored small ball. Chris Taylor of the Dodgers hit one home run in his first three seasons and then hit 21 in 2017. I think he would've been the World Series MVP had the Dodgers beaten the Astros. He's a good outfielder and he can play the infield too. The Dodgers have a few guys like that. The catcher, Austin Barnes, can also play in the infield, which is great. That's some flexibility for Dave Roberts to have as manager.

I think the relievers in the 2017 Astros-Dodgers World Series were the worst in the history of the World Series. The worst. Maybe that's why so many were used, because they all stunk. The Astros wouldn't even use their closer, Ken Giles, with a lead late in games by the end of the series. And they still won.

And the Astros won with Josh Reddick playing every game. He was 1-25 in the ALCS, and then he went 4-24 in the World Series. I would've benched him at some point. I couldn't believe they kept playing him, although he did hit .314 in the regular season, and he is a good outfielder with a strong arm. I was surprised Cameron Maybin didn't play more, although I think Maybin could be more aggressive as a player. But at least he puts the ball in play. Reddick was terrible at the plate, and he was throwing his equipment after at-bats. Why didn't they use Carlos Beltran more?

Getting back to the bullpen, there were very few impressive relievers. Brendan Morrow pitched in all seven World Series games and did well in all but one of them. The guy that really impressed me was Charlie Morton. I always pull for the underdog anyway. Morton was 46-71 in the National League but then came to the Astros and went 14-7 and he won Game 7 of the ALCS. He pitched so well in the last game of the World Series. He was so emotional after Houston won it all. He had an up-and-down career but he really has some control. He knows how to pitch and he's not afraid to pitch inside. They had a few guys struggling. Ken Giles lost his spot as closer. Will Harris scuffled as well.

The managing was a big deal in the 2017 World Series. In Game 2, Rich Hill was taken out after giving up one run in four innings and striking out seven batters. That meant the closer had to get six outs instead of three, and the Dodgers blew the lead in the ninth and lost in extra innings. Atta boy, Dave Roberts.

The game is run by statistics too much, way too much. They assume a few times through the lineup the other team will start hitting him. Well, let the other team actually start hitting them. And Hill got ticked off when they took him out in Game 6, and he had a right to be ticked off. These guys don't manage from their hearts and brains, they look at the statistics the front office throws at them. "You've got to do this, this and this." That's not managing. Managers today are like robots. They're taking orders from the front office and these computer geeks who have all the statistics. And this is the probability of this happening, and that happening. If you gave that to Billy Martin he would've laughed in your face and burned them. Gil Hodges would've been nice about it but would've said, "I don't think so." The idea that you need a new reliever every time through the lineup is tough, because now you're asking four or five pitchers to put up zeroes as opposed to two or three. They can't give up anything. And everybody has to be on. These starters have no chance to pitch deep into games unless you're talking about Justin Verlander or Clayton Kershaw. I would've thrown Yu Darvish in there but he couldn't make it out of the second inning in both of his World Series starts.

Joe Buck made a point on Fox during Game 7 that A.J. Hinch was trusting his eyes. Charlie Morton pitched the last four innings and picked up the win. So Hinch wasn't looking at all the statistics when Morton was in there. He knew what the situation was, and saw that Morton was pitching well. It was the opposite of "Robot" Roberts, as I call the Dodger manager. These guys really are robots. How about understanding the flow of the game? It's been taken over by statistics and these front office geeks who have never played a game in their life but they're experts on computers, and analyzing this, and analyzing that. There's has to be a time when you go with your heart and trust what you see, and what you know about your players. It's very frustrating to watch these managers "manage."

Gil Hodges would be laughing from Heaven if he saw how these guys were managing today.

Managing in the majors is tough. If there was one guy I could pick to run a team in today's game it would be Joe Girardi. He's a class guy, a smart guy. I have no idea why the Yankees let him go after being one win away from the World Series. He's a good manager and I thought they would keep him with all the young kids they have on the team. Some reports said he didn't communicate enough. Come on. Earl Weaver would hardly talk to his players. Gil Hodges was able to win without yelling at us or laughing with us. Some guys are stoic and are successful at it. Walt Garrison, the old Cowboys fullback, was asked if head coach Tom Landry ever smiled. "I don't know, but I've only been here nine years."

The Red Sox fired John Farrell after he won the division two straight years, and the Nationals did the same thing to Dusty Baker. Baker wasn't too happy about it. What do you have to do to keep your job? If you don't win the World Series, there's a chance you're going to be fired. It's a young man's game. It was funny when Alex Cora was the Astros bench coach and every team wanted him as manager. He could turn out to be very good, but he had no managing experience and he was more sought after than guys who have led teams to playoffs. (Manager Alex Cora won the 2018 World Series with the Boston Red Sox.)

Now teams want more communication. Gil Hodges didn't talk to us a lot. So what? He knew we knew how to play the game and we did know the game. We made very few mental errors. To me, it is obvious that most of these players in today's game do not know how to play the game. A manager doesn't talk to his players enough? Poor darlings.

Mission Viejo, as well as most of California, has a lot of those kids. To me, Southern California has the best athletes in the world. Pick your sport: golf, swimming, water polo, baseball, football, tennis, soccer. There are people who move out here because of the talent, coaching, and the weather. A lot of these kids go on to get scholarships to play college ball out of state, and they're back within a year. I call them the Mission Viejo Darlings. They can't be away from mommy and daddy for too long. I've seen it so many times over the years, and these kids are good athletes. They're playing for national programs, but they miss California and they come back here.

The problem with today's game is that they let the brain get in the way. You can't overthink when you're hitting. That ball is on you in a split-second, and you have to have a plan before the guy throws the ball. But today's managers have all these notes. Watch the old Mets games and see how calm Gil Hodges was just sitting there. He was probably churning inside, but he was sitting there next to Rube Walker, our pitching coach. He didn't have any notes but he was a great manager.

Something else I noticed is catchers picking up a ball in the dirt with their mitts. It's just sitting there and they pick it up with their glove hand. Infielders and outfielders do it too. I've seen it happen so many times, where they'll try it and the ball pops out of the glove. You have to barehand the ball. Even if it just rolls a little, use the bare hand, not the glove hand. Once you pick it up with the glove, you still have to transfer it to your bare hand, and that might be the difference in a runner taking the next base. I remember one game when I was coaching Little League, there was a ball hit to our first baseman. He dropped it, and then picked it up with his glove, which is tough to do with that big glove that first baseman use. Even though it was in the middle of the game, I called timeout and went out there. I said, "Give me the ball." The kids knew what I was going to do. I put it on the ground, and I told him to pick it up correctly. He picked it up with his bare hand. I mean, I stopped a game over this. Little things like that are important to learn.

A strange play ended the Yankees-Indians ALDS. Aroldis Chapman got Edwin Encarnacion looking at strike three to end the series. Gary Sanchez, the New York catcher, dropped the ball but never tagged the batter. Nobody seemed to notice except me and Todd Frazier, the third baseman, who told Sanchez to tag him. It didn't matter because Encarnacion didn't bother running to first base and gave himself up. Why wouldn't you at least run to first and force the throw?

Teams can win or lose games on third strikes being dropped. Remember in Game 2 of the 2005 ALCS, AJ Pierzynksi went to first after a dropped strikeout by the catcher that would have ended the inning had he not run to first. The White Sox scored the winning run a batter later. The Angels catcher just rolled the ball back to the mound instead of tagging Pierzynksi, although they thought they didn't have to because it never hit the ground according to the Angels. But you can't assume, and you always have to hustle. There were games, even in the postseason, where a batter would be jogging because he assumed a ball would be caught and was on first instead of second when the ball fell in.

You can't try to break up a double play anymore, unless the infielder is standing there and not moving at all. During the World Series, one of the Astros made a routine slide into Chase Utley, and the play was reviewed on video replay to see if it should be interference. What was a normal play years ago is now looked at on replay. And you can't try to break up a play at home and take out the catcher. But the catcher has to be real careful about what they do about blocking the plate. There was an NLCS game where the Cubs catcher was called for blocking the plate and the Dodgers were awarded a run. Joe Maddon got ejected over that one. Catchers get called for having a foot across the plate when they're waiting for the throw? The catchers have to think about where they'll be before the throw gets there so that they won't be penalized by the umpire. That's one of the frustrating things about watching the game today.

Instead of throwing four balls for an intentional walk, they let the guy go to first. The powers to be think that speeds the game up? That takes away from the game. How many pitchers over the years have thrown wild pitches while issuing an intentional walk? During the 1972 World Series, Johnny

Bench was up and the Oakland catcher put his glove out for an intentional walk but then jumped back in and they struck out Bench. It takes away a lot of strategy. And what if the guy accidentally throws it over the plate? Miguel Cabrera won a game a few years back with a single when the Orioles were trying to put him on base.

Is that how they want to speed up the game? Come on. Give me a break. What they should do is stop those catchers and pitchers to meet every pitch. They have so many meetings at the mound in one inning. That would speed it up big time. You don't see the top pitchers in the game meeting up after every pitch. It looks to me like pitchers don't want to pitch. It's like they're afraid especially these relievers. It's like they're afraid to throw the ball and they keep needing the catcher to come to the mound. There are times the pitcher will throw over to a base when it's completely unnecessary, almost as if they're just trying to put off delivering the actual pitch. They're very timid, and you can't be timid playing the game of baseball.

Games take so long that they started putting commercials in between at-bats. Fox went to a split screen of the game and a commercial throughout the series. I guess they have to do what television and the sponsors tell them to do.

The pitchers take so long to deliver a pitch. If I'm a hitter, when a pitcher is getting the ball and throwing it, in my mind he has confidence and knows what he's doing. There's no doubt. Whatever the catcher puts down, they're going to throw that pitch. They're in sync. As an outfielder, I wanted the pitchers to work quickly. There were times that I would be in centerfield and I would yell, "Throw the f------ ball" if I thought he was taking too long. It drove me nuts. Why don't these managers tell the slow pitchers that the fielders are more alert when the game is moving along at a good pace?

It was nice to see Dallas Keuchel give credit to his pitching coach, Brent Strom, in an interview. I played ball with Brent in the California Collegiate League, and then we later played in the minors together. What a great job he did with that staff. Brent is one of the nicest guys in the world, and I'm so happy for him.

Funny how I used to try to knock the ball out of a pitcher's glove, and now a runner just lets the pitcher tag him and pat him on the butt. I used to try to run through them, but if someone did that now they would be ejected. The game is a lot softer, with a capital S. And it's going to get softer down the road. I would love to see another Roger Clemens, or Tom Seaver, or Nolan Ryan. Or those Astros teams with Larry Dierker I used to face. I wouldn't be digging in down 0-2 or 1-2. We were leery up there, which takes away from your hitting.

The baseball pension plan is probably one of the best in the country, other than the ones politicians give themselves. But it's tough to beat the Major League Baseball players' pension. I think a guy has to play 40 days now in the majors to qualify. It's incredible. But this really starts with guys who came up after 1980. What about the guys who played in the decades before? They gave a pension to Negro League players who never played in the Major Leagues...why not the guys who played in Major Leagues in the '50s, '60s, and '70s. There are not many guys left who played in the 1950s. But why not give some more pension money to the older players. It's terrible. It's not even going to cost Major League Baseball that much money to take care of these older ballplayers who played before the 1980 deadline. I'm in my 70s, and there are guys older than me out there. And there are younger guys who didn't play the necessary time to qualify for a full time pension. That should be corrected. A lot of those guys are hurting. They got out of the game and didn't have anything. BAT, the Baseball Assistance Team, does a lot for retired players who were down and out as they got older.

I'm a blessed man. God has blessed me with Sheridan. I have five wonderful children, and 10 (and counting) beautiful grandchildren. And I was a member of one of the most unforgettable and one of the best baseball teams of all time: the 1969 World Series champion New York Mets. And I have the ring to prove it. How can you beat that?

Acknowledgments

I would like to thank John Tormey for suggesting David Russell to contact me. When David did contact me, I wasn't exactly thrilled about the idea of a book. I asked him, Why me? I wasn't a Tom Seaver or Nolan Ryan. I was just one of 26 guys on one of the most unforgettable teams of all time. But that is who he wanted to write about, one of the "other guys." Tormey mentioned to David that I might be an interesting subject. After a number of months, David's persistency paid off and the book idea became a project. I thank David for hanging in there with me. He is quite a young man.

To Art Shamsky for his foreword, and Keith Olbermann, Jerry Koosman, Bobby Pfeil and Ron Swoboda for taking the time to write a few lines for the book. To Mary Vaccaro for the layout of this book and Nick Hirshon for proofreading the manuscript. And Baseball-Reference.com for being a guide for fact-checking and statistics.

Made in the USA
Coppell, TX
16 July 2021

59037497R00134